practicing discernment
with youth

YOUTH MINISTRY ALTERNATIVES

---

practicing discernment with youth

a transformative youth ministry approach

david f. white

THE
PILGRIM
PRESS
Cleveland

The Pilgrim Press, 700 Prospect Avenue,
Cleveland, Ohio 44115-1100, U.S.A.
thepilgrimpress.com

10 09 08 07 06 05   5 4 3 2 1

Library of Congress Cataloging-in-Publication Data

White, David F., 1955-
    Practicing discernment with youth : a transformative youth ministry approach /
David F. White.
        p.   cm. – (Youth ministry alternatives)
    Includes bibliographical references.
    ISBN 0-8298-1631-3 (pbk. : alk. paper)
    1. Church work with youth. 2. Discernment (Christian theology) 3. Christian
youth – Religious life.   I. Title.   II. Series.

BV4447.W532 2005
259'.23 – dc22
                                                        2004063452

Contents

Preface   vii

Acknowledgments   xiii

Introduction: Putting youth ministry in its place   3

Part one
Discernment as an approach
to youth ministry

1. The social construction of adolescence and the vocation of youth:
   A theological vision for youth ministry   13

2. Cultural forces and the crisis in contemporary youth ministry   35

3. Reclaiming the Christian practice of discernment   63

Part two
Practicing discernment
in your setting

4. Listening: Loving God with your heart — Movement one   89

5. Understanding: Loving God with your mind — Movement two   114

6. Remembering and dreaming: Loving God with your soul —
   Movement three   138

7. Acting: Loving God with your strength — Movement four   174

8. Appropriating discernment for ministry with youth   200

Preface

The Youth Theological Initiative (YTI) is a center for research and education, based at Candler School of Theology, Emory University, whose goal is to reconceive the way youth are viewed within society and within the church. The Youth Theological Initiative began as a dream of Dr. Craig Dykstra of the Lilly Endowment many years ago. He had a hunch that teenagers needed a place to address questions of a theological nature that were not being adequately addressed in their local congregations. A grant to create such a place was provided to the Candler School of Theology, and in the summer of 1993 Dr. Don Richter became YTI's first director. Under the current leadership of Dr. Faith Kirkham Hawkins and Dr. David F. White, YTI has engaged in an active program of education and research, exploring questions of how congregations can more adequately engage young people as Christian disciples in the fullest sense.

Discipleship, as fostered through YTI's work, is characterized by a multifaceted commitment to acting in the world as Jesus acted, rather than merely identifying with Jesus as one's "personal" savior. Woven together within disciples' lives are practices and commitments following the model offered to the church by Jesus. Discipleship requires *attentiveness to the holy,* that is, to God's ongoing activity in the world. It requires *prophetic social critique,* engendered by seeing the world as God sees it and speaking out for that vision. Discipleship in its fullest sense also requires *justice-seeking action* in the world on behalf of "the widows and orphans" and the neediest of God's children. These practices are partnered with *compassionate responses to all creation,* the powerful and the oppressed, in the awareness that all are beloved of God. And Christian discipleship in its fullest sense includes *a commitment to transformative, mutual relationships* among all people, so that all participants in those relationships are brought into closer relationship with God and greater congruence with the *imago dei* within each one.

YTI's efforts to foster this kind of full discipleship are centered in the YTI Summer Academy, an ecumenical four-week program in justice-seeking theological education for seniors in high school from across the United States. The goal of the academy is to equip young persons to engage in theological reflection and action, and so to ignite their vocational imagination as "public theologians" for the benefit of church and society.

In addition to the Summer Academy, YTI's work includes a twofold agenda of research and assessment, along with public interpretation and education. As a result, the Initiative has become an internationally recognized leader in alternative approaches to youth ministry and research in the theological practices and perspectives of youth. Representatives from YTI are regularly consulted in conversations with denominational leaders and international associations that study youth ministry.

The need for a project like YTI, and for alternative visions of youth ministry, grows out of the recognition that for three decades the task of conceptualizing youth ministry has largely been left to independent commercial enterprises that have failed to recognize the importance of denomination, theology, ethnicity, class, and other cultural particularities for shaping Christian discipleship. In addition, youth ministry as it has evolved over these decades lacks significant critique of the shift in the social roles of young people in the second half of the twentieth century and into the twenty-first century, in which youth are increasingly ghettoized as passive consumers rather than treated as agents of faith influencing the common good.

Decades of domestication, marginalization, and trivialization of youth ministry by theology schools, denominations, and publishing houses has distorted our imagination of what counts as youth ministry. The image of youth ministry as trivial, spectacle, or pragmatic has left many hungry for youth ministry approaches that include social critique and engagement, theological sophistication, faith formation, and a genuine knowledge of and respect for the unique youth of today. The Youth Ministry ALTERNATIVES series has been jointly conceived by The Pilgrim Press and David F. White and Faith Kirkham Hawkins of the Youth Theological Initiative to address that hunger.

The Youth Ministry ALTERNATIVES series aims to clearly articulate approaches to youth ministry that embody social awareness and theological reflection and foster the distinctive gifts of youth for the church and the world. The series will highlight approaches to youth ministry that embody the following commitments:

1. **Dialogue with Living Communities.** This series will highlight approaches for fostering dynamic dialogue between the Christian traditions and youth and adults in living communities of faith.

2. **Deeper Understanding.** This series will engage this dialogue to deepen understanding of youth, theology, and youth ministry. Of particular interest is the wisdom emerging from a variety of underexplored sources that will be identified and interpreted, including the following:

   - the wisdom of youth

   - the wisdom of communities engaged in youth ministry

   - the contexts of youth, including their inner landscapes, communities, cultures, and physical environments

   - the resources of Christian tradition

3. **Transformative Practices.** From these conversations and the wisdom gleaned from youth, communities, and their contexts, this series will especially highlight a range of practices for engaging youth in ministry, such as:

   - doing theology and ministry with youth

   - taking youth seriously — their wounds, blessings, and gifts

   - mobilizing and enhancing youth agency and vocation

- enhancing formation and transformation of youth as they journey in faith
- articulating clear approaches to youth ministry
- discerning a congregation's unique youth ministry

•

Practicing Discernment with Youth: A Transformative Youth Ministry Approach inaugurates the series. This book is about one thing — *inviting young people to be Christian disciples.* Surely this is a simple enough aim, shared by countless youth ministers, families, and congregations. But for those deep inside the world of youth ministry — those who have practiced youth ministry for decades, write curriculum for youth, identify trends in adolescence and faith development, or articulate new strategies for youth ministry — accomplishing this aim is no longer as simple as it once seemed.

The context of youth ministry has changed in some dramatic ways. Youth ministry once understood itself as supplementing and supporting the nurture provided by culture — by family, school, state, and community — but recent shifts have set cultural norms and values at odds with the Christian faith. Specifically, cultural expectations about what counts as worthwhile lifestyles, vocational choices, and preparation for such lifestyles and vocations have become the elephant in many church youth rooms — rarely acknowledged, but around which every youth ministry activity must tiptoe. This culture prefers that young people be compliant in school in order to secure a credential necessary for future — preferably lucrative — employment, largely unaware of the workings of the world, and logics other than the logic of the market. Most of all, this culture prefers that our young people be passive consumers of its goods.

These cultural expectations instilled by the omnipresent commercial media and reinforced by parental fear and simple good wishes for their young people have prompted a great deal of confusion in youth ministry. Questions central to youth ministry prompted by this cultural shift include the following:

- What counts as Christian formation? Should youth ministers stick to teaching Bible stories and abstract moral principles, or should we teach young people to discern among the choices offered by culture and act in the ways that Jesus might?

- What is adolescence? Is adolescence merely a preparatory stage for real life that will begin some time following college, grad school, or when one has all the important possessions — or are young people capable of engaging the world critically and creatively now?

- What does it mean to be a disciple of Jesus Christ? Is a disciple one who identifies with Jesus or one who acts in the world as Jesus acted?

- How should young Christians relate to this postmodern culture? Should young people accept or reject the ever-expanding range of commercial and entertainment products?

These issues are not often engaged by popular youth ministry, but raise important questions about the situation of contemporary adolescents, deeply influenced by demands and seductions of American life that increasingly limit space allowed for the gospel and its concern for "love of God and neighbor." Like the fish that is presumably the last to recognize the water in which it exists, youth ministers have for a long time unreflectively worked amidst assumptions about what constitutes normal youth and ministry. We live in a culture — like all cultures — that exerts pressures upon us to validate some social roles and not others. This book raises questions about these culturally validated roles, specifically about what is appropriate for young people, and proposes an approach to youth ministry that takes seriously culture, theology, and the gifts and capacities of youth.

The future of youth ministry, as is argued in this book, must include equipping youth and congregations with skills for bringing the gospel into creative tension with the particular questions and circumstances of our lives and those of our youth — including questions of lifestyle, vocation and social responsibility. If youth ministries are to resist the cultural influences that dilute the power and hope of the gospel, we need to recover practices of discernment that bring the gospel into conversation with our lives and the culture in which we move.

This book presents an approach to youth ministry that draws upon Christian practices of discernment. Discernment, as articulated in this book, awakens the best in young people — their hearts, minds, souls, and bodies — and offers means for them to find their way in their dance with the Holy. In this book, youth and congregations are introduced to the organic rhythms of discernment that include ancient and modern practices of *listening, understanding, dreaming, and acting*. These rhythms are introduced as ways to connect their lives with God's and neighbors' and to lift their hearts, minds, souls, and bodies into the fullness envisioned by the gospel, as ways of healing their own broken selves and the wounds of the world.

Young people are surrounded by distractions of popular culture that drown out the invitation to walk as disciples of Jesus. This book is about teaching young people to listen and respond to what they hear within and without, to the cries of the suffering, to the broken heart of God, and to their own yearning to speak and act.

DAVID F. WHITE AND FAITH KIRKHAM HAWKINS
Series editors, Youth Theological Initiative
Candler School of Theology, Emory University

Acknowledgments

Lest anyone think that writing a book is a simple matter of putting fingers to a keyboard, let me suggest that for some of us writing is instead a bit like constructing an edifice, a bit like giving birth, and a bit like breathing. Like building a house, writing entails a process of laying foundational ideas and creating an argument around those ideas. Yet in writing books, building materials are not simply at hand, but require contemplative space into which ideas can emerge. Like giving birth, books cannot be rushed, but they gestate in the recesses of our souls until ready to be born. And like breathing, books are only partly the products of deliberation and intention, but are also influenced by accidents such as friendships, interests, and passions — those things that touch us in such a way that we find our lives cannot not be about them.

I take great pleasure in expressing gratitude to the many persons whose intentional and accidental contributions were breathed into this work, and especially those whose friendship made space safe enough for these ideas to be born. I especially want to thank my teachers and colleagues at the Claremont School of Theology, Dr. Frank Rogers and Dr. Mary Elizabeth Moore. My friends and colleagues at the Youth Theological Initiative at Candler School of Theology deserve special mention, especially Dr. Brian Mahan, who bore the onerous burden of reading early drafts and challenged me to think of the importance of writing well. I miss our meetings at local cafés over legal pads and scribbled napkins. I also want to thank Dr. Michael Warren at St. John's University, whose own books opened for me a new universe of possibilities for youth and ministry. Thank you also to Stacia Brown and David Purdum, who gave important feedback on the style and substance of this book.

Over my thirty-some-odd years of ministering with young people, a number of congregations stand out as important in my own formation as Christian, minister, and scholar. Thank you to Pascagoula First United Methodist Church and Galloway United Methodist Church in Mississippi. Thank you also to Anchor Park United Methodist Church in Anchorage, Alaska. And thank you to First United Methodist Church in Upland, California. Thank you to my lifelong friends, Rev. Billy Still, Rev. James Loftin, and Rev. Tommy Artmann, whose friendships have sustained me since our own adolescence all those years ago.

A grant from the Religion Division of the Lilly Endowment provided funding for the Youth Discipleship Project at the Claremont School of Theology, giving me the opportunity to explore these ideas with young people and congregations over three years from 1998 to 2001. Thank you to Craig Dykstra and Chris Coble, who took a great risk in inaugurating the Theological Programs for High School Youth. I consider this present writing to be a final report on our work to the Lilly Endowment and hereby express my lasting thanks for its generous help.

Finally, special thanks go to my wife, Melissa Wiginton, who never seemed to tire of hearing me articulate these ideas, giving me confidence that someone else might also find them helpful. This book is dedicated to my family, James Loyd, Jonell, Kathy, Susan, Chris, Matthew, Jamie, and Katie. With this host of witnesses I celebrate the completion of this book and offer it to you.

practicing discernment
with youth

Introduction

Putting youth ministry in its place

A decade or so ago, as a youth minister in Anchorage, Alaska, I awoke some winter mornings to frequently find small cars buried beneath enormous snowbanks. On such mornings, I sometimes, on my way to work, drove past a school bus stop filled with bleary-eyed teenagers steeling themselves against the cold and the coming school day. One particular morning and for several thereafter, my attention was drawn to the unusual spectacle of a group of teenage boys standing in the cold, wearing penny loafer shoes . . . and no socks! While every other sane Alaskan was wearing calf-height, fur-lined boots or their equivalent, with several layers of woolen socks, these young rebels were sockless and shivering, their feet protected by mere thin strips of leather designed more for style than warmth. I was confused by their odd choice of footwear until a father, whose son was among the boys standing at the bus stop, told me that a favorite television program among this group of peers was *Miami Vice,* a popular television program of the late 1980s in which two stylish detectives in sports cars solved crimes to the beat of techno-pop music. One of these detectives was known for wearing colorful T-shirts beneath sport coats . . . and no socks! My friend quipped philosophically, "Our boys are adopting *Miami Vice* style in an Alaska climate."

In effect, the imaginations of these boys were cut loose from their Alaskan context and floating free among the balmy Florida images provided by the entertainment culture. Our boys were distracted from a deep sense of place — geography, history, tradition, culture, experience, and climate — that seems important, partly for survival in a locality like Alaska, and seduced by images of a quite different place. Such seduction is understandable, particularly on subzero mornings, but it also inhibits their appreciation of the beauty, history, culture, blessings, and wounds of Alaskan life, and the development of the wisdom necessary to negotiate the complexities of this place and to participate with God in celebrating and transforming it. As one who grew to appreciate the beauty Alaska — to such an extent that I became an amateur Native culture enthusiast, historian, skier, mountaineer, sailor, hiker, and landscape painter, within the sublime mountains, forests, glaciers, seas, and people — it saddened me to witness this seduction of our youth away from this place.

While the above seduction describes the contemporary situation of many young people across the breadth of our culture of entertainment, a similar seduction also constitutes the situation of popular youth ministry. Congregational youth ministry over the last half-century has undergone a seduction or abstraction from its own sense of place — from a sense of local history, indigenous theological perspectives, material conditions of particular communities, and the idiosyncratic wounds and signature gifts of local youth. Today, like Alaskan boys with *Miami Vice* style, the expectations and imaginations of congregations about youth ministry are as likely to originate in Southern California, Colorado, or denominational headquarters, as in their particular communities or congregations. Youth ministry in the United States was once all but abandoned, left waiting at the bus stop by mainline Protestant denominations that a half century ago diverted resources to other areas, by theological schools that saw little importance in reflecting on the distinctiveness of work with adolescents, and by congregations that delegated youth ministry to paid professionals. Abandoned by its proper guardians — those more representative of its particular theological traditions and social contexts — youth ministry was left to roam from pillar to post, from parachurch organizations to youth ministry resource organizations-cum-corporations that eagerly accepted the role of surrogate parent — supporting, educating, and forming the imagination of local congregations, and ensuring the survival of youth ministry. The responsibility of developing the theory and practice of youth ministry shifted away from congregations, denominations, and their theological centers to these distant authorities.

We should be grateful for the development of youth ministry theory and practice over three decades under the surrogacy of these authorities. However, while youth ministry constructed by distant sources has given order and purpose to the chaos of youth ministry, for many congregations these celebrated models of youth ministry have never quite fit. These extracontextual models have left congregations ill equipped to negotiate the problems and possibilities of adolescents in their particular contexts. The models have left the adolescents' feet cold.

Popular youth ministry in its worst forms leaves young disciples ill equipped to engage the powers and principalities that encompass adolescent life, fostering instead an abstract Christian identity that knows little of the wounds or blessings of their particular world. There is no such thing as Christian discipleship in general, but Christian faith and practice require incarnation in particular times and places. For too many Christians, their faith is held as a romantic abstraction focused on deep personal beliefs or a world beyond, but ignores how the Spirit is working within history, and how all of creation (including their neighborhood) is groaning for transformation. Such a view splits Christian faith off from the wounds and blessings of the world, relegating faith to one sphere and life to another — rarely allowing the two to converse. As long as the gospel remains an abstraction or a mere set of romantic ideas, we risk ignoring the particular ways this world is distorted — including how young people are marginalized, exploited, and alienated by various social structures — and we cannot become partners with God in transforming this world in the way Christ intended.

If Christian faith is to be more than an idea floating above the earth, or an appendage stapled to the edge of a life lived unreflectively in obeisance to other forces such as consumerism, racism, sexism, nationalism, or various ideologies and political influences, then there is a great need to identify practices through which young people may connect their life world to the life of God. In short, local contexts in all their complexity require that youth ministry take different shapes and focus on different theological themes according to the gifts and needs of particular youth and their unique communities. These particular forms are difficult to anticipate from a distance or in general, but require that local congregations gain skills for negotiating a sense of place and the particular ways the Spirit is moving in that place.

To gain a sense of place, congregations need to engage their young people in practices that resemble the discernment practiced by Christian communities throughout history, engaging the gifts and problems of their context through experience, reflection, discussion, and prayer, bringing their lives more fully into partnership with God's work. While various Christian movements have generated their own approaches to discernment, some of the most prominent practices include Ignatian contemplative practices; Quaker practices of clearness, consensus-building, and silence; biblical reflection that emerged from Protestant reformation; and the social analysis of Latin American base communities. These practices have in common their intent to explore decisions they face in their context, clarifying them in the light of God's wisdom. In this book, I develop the notion of practicing discernment among youth as a means of returning the responsibility for youth ministry to local congregations and youth groups, and as a way of responding to the particular wounds, blessings, and charisms of youth and congregations.

The importance of engaging youth in practicing discernment goes beyond the value of engaging their world more decisively on behalf of God. Viewing practices solely in terms of utility is always a risk in our utilitarian culture. In reality the practice of discernment, like all Christian practices, also has important internal goods — goods that accrue even apart from the ends they accomplish. In particular, the practice of discernment includes internal benefits that outweigh the convenience of downloading youth ministry approaches from distant sources. But the actual activities involved in the practice of discernment hold their own delights and strengths. In his book *Transforming Our Days,* Richard Gaillardetz argues that technology such as automatic dishwashers or microwave ovens saves us time and energy, but also removes us from other goods such as camaraderie, cooperation, humor, and goodwill that are present when families cook or clean dishes together. Another example involves the habit of eating fast food, in which we lose the benefit of sitting at table together with family, friends, or strangers, offering thanks to God, acknowledging the goodness of the earth and the workers that provided the food, and sharing the stories of our lives with each other.

Along with the convenience of adopting generalized youth ministry approaches from central organizations, we are sacrificing important benefits, including but not limited to conversation, conflict, and understanding between youth and adults; acknowledging the passions and gifts of youth; fostering delight in their human capacities of heart, mind, soul, and body; the deep social and theological insight that comes through collaborative struggle; and a unified church membership mobilized in action as witnesses for Christ in the world (the kind of unity that only comes on the other side of prayer, struggle, and conflict). Just as there are goods internal to practices of cooking, feasting, and cleaning that are lost when these practices are automated, there are also important internal benefits for congregations who engage together in discernment, benefits that are lost when youth ministry theory and practice are simply appropriated from a distant source. Congregations, adults and youth, who engage each other in discernment — in telling and hearing each other's stories, understanding the world in which youth are formed, and seeking to know how God calls them to respond in the world — find that in discerning together, they are in fact doing much of the work of youth ministry (and adult ministry).

The practice of discernment has historically been viewed as a means of resolving particular dilemmas that arise — whom to join in marriage, which career to pursue, whether or not to relocate to another city. However, this book introduces the practice of discernment as a more inclusive rhythm of life, involving not only dilemmas of which we are aware, but also a deliberate habit of raising to consciousness the preconscious tensions and contradictions inevitable in human life, especially in cultures hostile to life and faith. Instead of an episodic practice of discernment, I am advocating a continual dance that brings our ever-expanding awareness of others and ourselves before our ever-expanding awareness of God — exploring these landscapes with our hearts, minds, souls, and bodies. While former understandings of discernment involved a practice instrumental in resolving a dilemma, this view of discernment focuses not only on some end or dilemma, but also upon a way of life and the delight or goods internal to discernment.

Dance is an especially good metaphor for describing this approach to discernment. Christian theologians utilize a term, "perichoresis" or "to dance around," that describes the inner life of the Trinity, in which each person of the Godhead interpenetrates and participates in the life of the other. Not only does this describe the inner life of the Trinity, but also God's work of creation and redemption. God's playful and healing life is woven into the fabric of all creation, within and beyond human life. Theologians tell us that through God's lively dance we are awakened to our true life and purpose, and we are called to extend ourselves to others, inviting them into this dance. Discernment is a way of engaging the dance with God, of bringing all that we are before God to be healed and transformed, of integrating and reconciling the disparate parts of our lives and our world.

This book is divided into two parts: part 1 provides a rationale for discernment as an approach to youth ministry, and part 2 elaborates the movements of discernment and how to practice discernment in your setting.

Chapter 1 characterizes the social construction of adolescence, including the movement of young people from rural agrarian to urban industrial capitalist economies, early theories of adolescence, the subsequent ejection of youth from industrial work, and their eventual relegation to high schools and popular culture. Chapter 1 also illumines the logic of progress and exploitation embedded in the construction of adolescence, and introduces contemporary ecological and theological ideas to articulate an alternate view of youth ministry that respects and cultivates the gifts of youth. Further, this analysis of adolescence as a potential gift for communities also reveals the shadow side of not honoring youth and their gifts — their increased alienation, apathy, and violence.

Chapter 2 explores how cultural forces marginalize youth and create tensions predominant in contemporary youth ministry, such as enthrallment of youth to consumerism, cultural versions of success, and burnout among youth ministers. This chapter points to the need for forms of youth ministry that reconcile youth and adults and mobilize the gifts of youth for communities and for the reign of God.

Chapter 3 introduces the practice of discernment, its development through history, and its use as an approach to youth ministry. Much that is contained in various historical practices of discernment — for example, Ignatius, Quakers, Protestant reformers, and Latin American base communities — is captured in the four movements of listening, understanding, remembering/dreaming, and acting. This chapter also argues for an approach to knowing that is more holistic and integrative and responsive to love of God and neighbor that draws out and unifies the human heart, mind, soul, and body.

Chapters 4 through 7 introduce the respective movements of discernment — listening, understanding, remembering and dreaming, and acting — as pieces of a whole educational process, but also as distinctive ways of spirituality that involve the various human capacities of heart, mind, soul, and body. These chapters elaborate theological rationales for the respective movements, but also include extended sections that describe various activities that foster listening, understanding, remembering and dreaming, and acting.

Chapter 8 draws from the four movements of discernment and suggests some practical ways of organizing congregational youth ministry around them.

G. Stanley Hall, the first modern theorist of adolescence, in 1904 argued that adolescents were uniquely curious, passionate, and alive — that adolescence was the "golden stage of life." But these golden energies of youth are not automatic and can be muted when young people are distracted by approaches that do not engage them in responding to the wounds and blessings of their world. Much popular youth ministry encourages the notion that energy, vitality, faith, and life must be pumped into young people — requiring that we create spectacles and enormous amounts of our money and energy. In reality, young people in partnership with the Spirit can provide enormous energy for the healing of the world. Importing approaches to youth ministry for congregations to consume unreflective of their context is dangerous for a number of reasons, but most tragically we risk ignoring or muting the signature gifts of youth. By normalizing this style of youth ministry, the culture and the church have but forgotten the possibilities for young people to be awakened and their power to awaken us to the joy and justice of the gospel. Key to cultivating these gifts is engaging youth in exploring their world, their hearts, and the depths of the holy, through the practice of discernment. This spiritual energy cannot simply be pumped into youth, but must be midwived forth from the deep and holy currents within them.

Part one

Discernment as an approach to youth ministry

One

The social construction of adolescence and the vocation of youth

A theological vision for youth ministry

In Mary Shelley's 1818 novel *Frankenstein,* a tormented doctor is obsessed with the possibility of creating human life. Dr. Frankenstein directs his ghouls to harvest body parts from fresh cadavers, which he stitches together and jolts to life. At times, we do not quite know what to make of his odd creation that alternately exhibits a fondness for flowers and sudden slips into violence. The monster is not a child, although he exhibits a childlike dependence on the doctor. Nor is he an adult, although his oversize body provides physical strength characteristic of adults. He is alive yet dead in so many ways — dead to compassion, love, and wonder. Like all monsters, this one is a disturbing mixture of qualities that aren't quite congruous. In due course, the monster, unappreciative of his origins, conducts a violent spree and threatens the local villagers, the doctor, and himself. Yet, despite his end he is a sympathetic figure: we can only imagine how his heart was moved as a child or a husband or a father, before his multiple deaths and unlikely resurrection.

Literary historians tell us that Shelley wrote this cautionary tale to warn of how the Industrial Revolution would force human life into unnatural and dehumanizing rhythms and relationships — leaving us, like Frankenstein's monster, alive, yet dead to what makes human life worth living. Prior to the late nineteenth and early twentieth century, workers had opportunities for humanizing and creative work and relationships, but new social arrangements reduced them to a desperate struggle for money. Workers no longer attuned to the needs of the earth or to human rhythms of rest, renewal, connection, or creativity, but instead to production schedules and cycles of the market. Whereas for centuries the church had stigmatized expressions of greed, industrial culture came to legitimate ambition focused on individual wealth and the exploitation of some, rather than the good of the community. Shelley was among a minority warning that an emphasis on commerce and industry would distort our relations with nature, labor, and the human community, and would ultimately erode our humanity. While few of us would wish to return to preindustrial life, it is worth considering what we have lost in the bargain. We can attribute to industrialization not only the blessings of technology, progress, and wealth for some, but also the scourges of violence, alienation, greed, degradation of the environment, fragmentation of the human community, and poverty for many. But further, as we will see, human life was reshaped by commercial values and we lost a sense of the integrity and goodness of each stage of development — including adolescence.

As Shelley predicted, the pressures of commerce and industry have over the last century distorted human development — with its stages of infancy, childhood, adolescence, adulthood, and older adulthood — forcing unnatural rhythms and relationships. While developmental theorists have elaborated on the psychological and physiological changes throughout human life, we are much less familiar with how life has been rationalized by the logic of the market. Long before Shelley wrote her cautionary tale, church bells in medieval villages began tolling the time for beginning work and for commercial transactions, thus introducing an artificial sense of time, away from the natural rhythms of the sun and the body or the common good. As the rhythms of the day, so were the stages of modern life influenced by the resounding needs of the market — including pressures to produce and consume, and to turn everything into a commodity for sale. The fetishization of money changed our appreciation of almost everything — work, human relationships, relationships with nature, and youth. Prior to the Industrial Revolution, children passed with relative ease into adulthood, given that their ability to work determined their status as adults. The work of pre-industrial young people, while strenuous, was at times fulfilling — connecting them to the earth, their creativity, the care and guidance of adults, and the common good of the community, and affording them a more central social role. Not until the Industrial Revolution was child work considered too harsh and were youth banished from the workplace. Today adolescents' entry to adulthood is interminably delayed by the demands of education, which functions in part to fit them for the market — as producers and consumers. In contrast with their earlier social roles, youth are now relegated to high schools and to media-driven peer culture that disconnect them from adult care and guidance, the common good, and many of their former contributions and commitments.

The social institution of adolescence, like Frankenstein's monster, is not natural. It was constructed from a conglomeration of ideas and practices that served the interests of marketers, employers, labor unions, educators, politicians, and the middle class — yet remained oblivious to the yearnings of youth to contribute their gifts to the common good, and the church that sought to call forth these charisms. Like Shelley's monster, the social institution of adolescence is not only tragic for how it distorts the natural energies of youth, but also for how it turns to dismember the human family. Adolescence has tragic consequences everywhere, not only in places like Columbine High School or urban communities where violence has become normal. The habits of the heart forged in the contexts of high school and media-driven peer culture do considerable violence to human flourishing. Habits, for example, of quiescence, consumption, political ignorance, apathy, frenetic activity, lack of curiosity, and lack of critical thought and creativity are now prominent not only among youth — but among many adults. These habits arrest many adults in a domesticated form of adolescence, and thus degrade communities that require informed, interested, and engaged citizens in order to flourish.

A glimpse of the history of youth can help us unravel the tangle of ideas constructed by society and normalized as the institution of adolescence. We will see how dramatically the experience and context of adolescent life has changed in modern history.

Preindustrial context of youth

It may surprise most readers to learn that prior to the twentieth century, young people were anything but passive consumers of history. David Farragut, the U.S. Navy's first admiral, had his first commission as a midshipman at ten years of age, and his first command of a vessel at age twelve.[1] Thomas Edison ran his own printing business at age twelve. The men who won the American Revolution were barely out of high school — Alexander Hamilton was twenty, Aaron Burr, twenty one; Lafayette, nineteen. What amounted to a college class rose up and struck down the British Empire.[2] These youthful American revolutionaries seemed to have a sense of power, curiosity, adventure, and creativity largely lacking in contemporary youth.

Not only were preindustrial young people in popular mythology and poetry — because of their beauty and creative energy — identified with spring and the rebirth of life, their social roles also engaged them in seeking justice and social renewal. This is illustrated a bit later in Delacroix's painting of the French Revolution, *Lady Liberty Leads the People,* in which Lady Liberty is led by young people. Young people were among those who in 1789 fomented revolution in Paris cafés and died in numbers on the barricades, with cries of "liberty, fraternity and equality," and who marched alongside their elders in the early industrial era demanding lower bread prices and higher wages. Before the middle of the nineteenth century many youth engaged in serious work, held significant social roles, and contributed to the social equilibrium. Throughout history we see young people shaping a better world, including roles in every major peace and justice, labor, civil rights, and environmental movement in modern history — and the various contemporary antiwar, anti-sweatshop and antiglobalization movements.

Contemporary context of youth

By the mid-twentieth century, "good" adolescents became identified with roles of education or "preparation" for adult work and future social significance. While this shift left them without social significance, it provided many with leisure time and discretionary dollars — opening them to exploitation by marketers and their current role as consumers of fashion and entertainment commodities. In one generation that came of age in the 1930s and the 1940s, the role of young people shifted from helping to provide for their families to draining their families' income on commodity purchases.

The removal of young people from public life has had other consequences that corrode human community. Whereas once the worlds of youth and adults were intertwined, today few adults have a relationship of any significance with a young person. Because youth are relegated to distant worlds of high school and peer culture, adult perceptions of them are largely limited to projections of our fears and desires, manipulated by the media. Mostly through the lens of our televisions or from the corners of our eyes, we view teenagers as objects of energy and beauty or danger and adventure. Marketers use images of beautiful and energetic youth to sell soft drinks and shampoo, and images of dangerous youth to sell movies and music. By identifying youthful beauty and energy with their saleable products, marketers hope to convince adult consumers that their products add adventure and prolong youthfulness. Marketing strategies that entice our consumption by promising passion and adventure are deliberate appeals to qualities repressed in the overmanaged lives of many American adults.

However, media images do not just sell products or entertain us. They also form our expectations about how the world is supposed to be and our place in it. When youth is portrayed as the most significant source of vitality, then elderly people are devalued. Media images are especially powerful among young people who are still coming to understand the significance of their life. Identification with cultural images sometimes put young people at risk, as, for example, when beauty is normalized as thinness and young women starve themselves emulating television images, and when young boys assault girls, drink to excess, drive recklessly, and die by the thousands in car wrecks emulating media images that normalize danger, violence, and disrespect of self and others. Our distance from youth and the prevalence of exploitative media portrayals of youth make it easy for adults to perceive young people as objects of desire or fear, without knowing them as real people. Healthy development for young people requires that they look to adults who know and validate them in appropriate ways. But when we reflect back to young people assumptions that we have internalized from media images of irresponsible, incapable, or dangerous youth, they live into our expectations and become further alienated from their best selves — and their historical vocation as youth.

Ironically, while media portrayals of youth remind adults how much we ache to feel young and alive, our official version of "good" adolescence actually relegates young people to passive roles as consumers and students. While adults are entertained and thrilled by media images of dangerous, outrageous, or rebellious youth, in this culture financial security actually requires that young people comply with demands to become competent and cooperative commodities for sale on the job market. For many underclass youth — whether because of inadequate resources or outright resistance — this is a price too high. By physically or emotionally dropping out of "adolescence," many underclass youth begin their long journey into another kind of economic-political marginalization.

This myth portraying a domesticated adolescence has seized our imaginations so that we cannot view "good" youth in any other way or recall their contributions in premodern times — in which youth were shapers of history and guardians of social equilibrium. What were once understood as natural energies of youth — questioning the status quo, seeking justice, challenging and creating new social structures — are now arguably relegated to the "bad" or shadow side of adolescence, as precocity, delinquency, or "trouble making." While it is too simple to suggest that "good" youth do not also give rein to these energies, they must at times be split off or suppressed when attempting to negotiate an increasingly harsh and competitive market economy. This economy forces them to focus on marketable careers instead of concerns like human flourishing and love of God and neighbor. Like Frankenstein's confused and lonely monster, adolescents are left wandering with a strange set of contradictory messages constructed by the media and market — "Adults love youthful energies that remind us of what we have left behind (although we resent youth for possessing such energy)," and "Youth must ignore their hearts and become what the market needs — for them to be compliant, productive, and consumptive."

Within the contours of these conflicting messages we can see adolescence, like Frankenstein's monster, at cross-purposes with themselves. We have already suggested that commercial and industrial forces created this monstrosity, but how did religious Americans so easily consent to such a bargain that compromised their religious sensibilities, their authority, youth's integrity, and the common good of their communities? Unlike Dr. Frankenstein's creation, which was never accepted by the community because the doctor could not make the monster appear normal, adolescence has been embraced as a fixture in American society. How was the normalization of adolescence accomplished? What ideas were utilized to make this creation appear normal and acceptable? What is the ideological heart of this monster, adolescence?

The ideological heart of the monster

While there was no Dr. Frankenstein who glommed together this artificial construction of adolescence, there were certainly individuals whose visions guided the process. The myth of modern adolescence was already taking shape by 1904 when G. Stanley Hall, the first American theorist of adolescence, asked the world to imagine adolescence as a great river flowing down a mountain, branching into ever smaller streams and rivulets, gradually dissipating as it reaches the sea. He insisted that these golden energies were being wasted in their unchecked drain into public life and therefore needed to be dammed up in order to harness their full potential — a metaphor drawn from the nascent hydroelectric industry and the public water works. If youth expend their energy too soon in carousing, dancing, sex, delinquency, work, or political activism, they might not have the energy that the emerging industrial nation required from their adulthood. Like his Austrian colleague Sigmund Freud and others, Hall understood vitality or "libidinal energy" as finite, not to be squandered. He asked teachers to imagine themselves as engineers, and challenged them to create great dams to forestall the precocious flow of adolescent energy and to harness it "for the purposes of American progress" — at a time when social Darwinism contributed to the fear that only the strongest nations would survive. Since Hall first theorized adolescence as a dissipating river, his scientific ideas have largely been discounted, yet their residue still informs our view of youth. When asked to imagine "good" adolescents, we are not likely to view them involved in politics or leadership roles in church or community. We have indeed created great dams to contain and channel youthful energy for purposes that serve neither the common good nor youth themselves, except in a projected future. In addition to high schools — the great bulwark of adolescent energy — the juvenile justice system and prisons restrain those who do not comply as good adolescents. Youth organizations distract youth with frivolous activity devoid of social or global awareness, while the fashion and entertainment industries forestall youthful energy by creating passive consumers.

The destabilization of adolescence

Much like Dr. Frankenstein, who paid a great price for his artificial creation, domestication of youthful energies also comes at a high price. Modern adolescence and the institutions supporting it have become increasingly unstable as adolescent energy has become difficult to control. For much of the twentieth century, the limits of adolescence were offset by its relatively brief duration, its economic payoff, and the numerous opportunities for young people to exercise social power. However, over the last thirty years the opportunities that once made adolescence bearable have become limited, leaving young people with fewer ways to act upon history. Let us explore six recent limitations that promote this destabilization.

1. Adolescence begins with an earlier puberty and extends longer than ever before — often beyond the age of thirty if we consider the sociological definition of adulthood as achieving a significant social role, marriage, and steady employment. In part, we can account for this prolongation by the increased pressure to obtain educational credentials — undergraduate and graduate degrees. This prolongation leaves youth in situations in which they have less than full power for longer than any other generation in history.

2. Adolescence is destabilized by the realization that the promises of education no longer hold the guarantee of middle-class security. This guarantee is threatened in part by the sheer numbers of young people competing for professional jobs and middle-class employment. While the costs and expectations of education have risen significantly, its real value has diminished. Many jobs that parents and grandparents held with only a high school diploma now require college or graduate degrees. Ironically, young people report that many corporate jobs secured after college could be easily managed without a college degree and with less than three weeks of on-the-job training! The expensive college degree, formerly the key to middle-class employment and lifestyle, has become a necessary but insufficient credential.

3. Uncertainty about the future includes uncertainty about the potential for upward mobility in the workplace. Whereas it was once possible with hard work and perseverance to eventually achieve advancement from low-skill jobs to upper-management positions, today the concentration of upper-level and lower-level jobs has thinned out middle-level jobs, effectively limiting possibilities for advancing within the corporate world. This "declining middle"

has concentrated wealth and opportunity among the middle-aged and seniors. This situation is mirrored in the political habit of communities to limit the means for young people to achieve upward mobility — by voting against school bond issues and for a low minimum wage. Sociologists Côté and Allahar reveal that the middle-aged and seniors have for more than thirty years consolidated their wealth and power at the expense of the young, enforcing a prolonged and anxious adolescence lacking certainty of a future in the middle class, burdened with huge amounts of student loan debt.[3]

4. Along with the anxiety and uncertainty of middle-class youth, underclass youth are stripped of their earning power as they must compete with labor exported to developing countries.

5. Destabilization of adolescence has been further catalyzed by states that misunderstand the nature of this crisis, and have reacted to the displacement of young people with more severe laws criminalizing behaviors of youth once considered experimental. More than fifteen states now prosecute as felonies offenses previously judged as juvenile misdemeanors, filling prisons to overflowing with displaced young people. In California the growth of prisons — one of the fastest-growing industries in the state and populated disproportionately by young people — is quickly outstripping this state's investment in its universities.[4]

6. Adolescence is further destabilized by the decline in the number of adult mentors and sponsors — a void now filled by the entertainment media, which ushers young people into a specious adulthood. Relegating youth to media-driven peer culture and isolating them from adult relationships and centers of adult influence leave youth with a vague yearning for more influence or social agency, but without the opportunities or skills that come through experience in negotiating complex practical and social problems. Without opportunity as agents and without adult mentors, young people often lack a sense of loyalty to social institutions that was characteristic of their parents and grandparents.

The yearning for agency, abandonment by adult mentors, and the resulting lack of loyalty are key dimensions of a social crisis. Not only are young people left without the resources of earlier generations, but an unwitting society also reaps the bitter fruits of inattention. So strong are the natural yearnings of youth to act in the world that normal developmental antipathies are intensified between young people and their adult gatekeepers — parents, teachers, police, youth ministers, and other agents of social control that Hall envisioned.

If youth were made for such limits, this increased control would be no problem, but youth seem hardwired to explore, experiment, passionately follow ideals, challenge, deconstruct, and re-create. And to limit such energy is bound to make the adolescent bargain (security first, passion later!) tenuous at best.

The instability of adolescence extends in subtle and dramatic ways to various spheres of American life — families, neighborhoods, schools, and churches. As the promise of middle-class security is denied to many and the structures intended to support youth fail, we see a shadow adolescence come into focus as many youth, even among suburban communities, refuse to be good adolescents. The protective bubble of adolescence, theorized by G. Stanley Hall as a way to conserve and channel youthful energy and extended by Erik Erikson as a time to allow for experimentation and validation, now leaves many young people to negotiate adulthood without resources afforded youth in better times. The structures created to hold the energies of youth have relegated young people to institutions in which they are expected to cultivate a future for themselves apart from resources of wise adults, extended families, and communities, and, indeed, from any practical experience of the real world.

Moreover, for those who succeed in navigating adolescence into the security of individual success, as prescribed by our culture, the competition they endure threatens to kill their souls and further alienate them from friends and communities. We seem to be systematically removing the support required for adolescents to achieve healthy integration as adults with communal responsibility — also important for Christian discipleship. The comfortable American myth of adolescence is cracking at the seams. The dams Hall envisioned to keep youth in their place come at a high price and are barely holding firm.

Fortunately, unlike Frankenstein's monster, adolescence is not sewn together by stitches, but is held together only by our understandings and expectations for youth. Although the market has distorted human life in general and adolescent life in particular, in the American context these dehumanizing outcomes are not determined, but depend on the compliance of citizens. The myth of adolescence can be examined and reconstructed by logic other than that of the market — one perhaps grounded in the logic of God.

Rethinking the monster

What should be the role of the church in this situation? Can we sit idle while the monster institution of adolescence harms itself and others? Can we simply watch the rising tide of cultural distortion from the confines of our churches, pretending that our feet are not getting wet, that we are not already swimming in it? Youth ministry cannot avoid functioning knowingly or unwittingly in relation to this cultural myth of adolescence — either in support of or in resistance to it. Youth ministry for much of the twentieth century supported the dominant myth of adolescence, affirming the expectations of preparing youth for an increasingly distant future — not so much to empower youth as agents of faith in the contemporary world, but as a holding environment awaiting a promised adulthood. We in youth ministry have been largely uncritical of the myth of adolescence that sees the suppression of adolescent energy as the natural way of things. But is that the best we can do? Are there other sources to draw upon for our myths? If the church is to have credibility and relevancy in the world, we cannot allow culture to unilaterally establish our perspectives that shape our understandings of ministry. We must instead mine our own resources for understanding youth and their potential. We must tell our own story.

The Christian tradition compels us to imagine fresh ways of valuing youth, independent of their relation to some productive or normative adulthood. How is the church called to exist in relation to the myth of adolescence? What is the logic of God in relation to youth? Most importantly for youth ministry, what is the vision of youth that drives our ministry? The Christian tradition does indeed provide an alternate story to fund our understanding of the authentic vocation of youth. What is our theology of adolescence, and what is our theological vision for youth ministry?

The beauty of God

A good place to start our theological reflection on God's desire for creation in general and youth in particular is with the nature and person of God. The Bible tells us that "God is love," but we sometimes quote this verse without grasping the depths of its truth. Christian theology tells us that love has its source in the very Trinitarian essence of God — a dynamic vulnerability, responsiveness, mutuality, and interrelationship between Father, Son, and Spirit. All that God is and does is an extension of this love at the heart of God. God's love draws all things into right relationship with God and creation. But this ingathering neither obliterates individuals by assimilating us into God, nor delivers us unchanged. The love of God transforms us and our relationships with each other and God. One way of thinking of this transformation is in terms of "God creating beauty that mirrors God's own beauty." In aesthetics, beauty names the extraordinary situation in which all parts exist in right proportion to the whole. The artist intuitively places elements in appropriate relationship to others — a *figure* takes prominence in relation to the *ground* of a painting, a color becomes brilliant alongside its complementary color, highlights become vivid in relation to shadows — all in order to represent the central theme of the artist's choosing. Beauty is a set of relationships between the parts and the whole that strikes us as appropriate, proportionate, and pleasing. The creative interplay of the parts that transform the whole, and the whole giving new significance to the parts, is not only the aim of art, but describes the love at the heart of God and the essence of God's transforming work in the world. Artists speak of beauty and theologians speak of reconciliation or salvation, but they are both expressing what happens when some person or thing yields itself in love and is appropriately moved to right relationships. Christians believe that this yielding and transforming love happens most perfectly in and through God — the source of all beauty and love.

Yet this complex of Trinitarian relationships does not close in upon itself but from this loving center created the world as an extension of this love. Creation was never intended to exist in isolation, but in order to satisfy its purpose the creature must also be caught up in the love of God, loving and being loved — transformed by love and called to love the world into beauty. The God of beauty created the world in beauty and invites all things to be caught up in a dance of beauty with a promise of greater beauty as God's reign is fulfilled. Although this beauty begun in God's very nature is woven into the very fabric of creation, the Hebrew scriptures reveal sin as a disruption of relationship between creation and Creator. But they also reveal God as one who seeks to draw all into (w)holiness or *shalom*. The story of Jesus continues the theme of God's reconciliation of a broken world. Jesus, true to his origins, gave himself in love unto death, but in his resurrection promised an ultimate reconciliation in the reign of God, where the lion shall lie peacefully with the lamb and all nations celebrate around a wedding table, utterly alive in God's beauty. Christian hope not only makes vivid its central theme, love of God, but those around the wedding table also find their humanity heightened while blended harmoniously in this eschatological symphony. Christians understand creation perfected in two ways, one by which the thing subsists in itself, the other by which it is ordered to other things proportionate to itself. Human fullness is best accomplished within the emerging beauty of human community, and human community flourishes as individuals contribute their gifts in right relationship to all others. And the creature increases its perfection — its distinctness and relatedness — as the creature and human community returns to right relationship with God. This is the hope of creation and of each creature — to return to God's beauty on earth as in heaven. The great affirmation of Christian hope is that as we shift the subject of our life and art to focus the beauty of God, our lives paradoxically take on greater beauty, clarity, and energy. In the Christian story, history ends as it is begun, in love, beauty, and fullness — as all creation returns from whence it sprang in God's love.

The ideal of wholeness/beauty infuses Christian theology from Jesus to contemporary theologians. Theologians have reminded us of often-forgotten aspects that contribute to this beautiful wholeness. Karl Barth and others reminded us that the beauty that we seek cannot be fulfilled in our human projects, but in the wholly otherness of God. Latin American liberation theologians have reminded us that the wholeness we seek in God must include the poor. Political theologians have reminded us that the wholeness of God's reign cannot forget the ways our political structures deter beauty. Feminist theologians have reminded us that this beauty must also include the gifts of women. Sallie McFague and others have called our attention to how Christian theology should include care for the earth. African American theologians point to the beauty revealed through the wounds and blessings of black people. The very scope of Christian theology reveals a rainbow of diverse gifts that God wishes to weave into beautiful wholeness.

Yet, the church of Jesus has largely ignored a dimension of the wholeness/beauty implied in the fullness of Christian hope — youth and their contributions to the reign of God. Our admittedly incomplete account of adolescence reveals disjunction between youth and their communities, their parents, and their own hearts, minds, souls, and bodies, such that our communities and our youth cannot fully reflect the beauty of God. In Christian theology, God's love seeks to create beauty — including bringing young people into right relationship with God, the human community, and their best selves. Theology that ignores the brokenness of youth or any among us forgets its roots in the love and beauty of God.

Erik Erikson, arguably the most important theorist of adolescence, saw beauty woven into the human life cycle. In addition to being a human scientist, Erikson was an artist whose aesthetic sensibilities were particularly suited for seeing the beauty of human life and community. For Erikson, beauty is manifested on many levels as the human life cycle progresses through stages of equilibrium, each with its own virtue, integrated with greater complexity as we mature. According to Erikson the various stages of human development cannot be thought of as discrete stages advancing toward some normative completion, but as overlapping and interrelating, parent with child, old with young, each contributing their gifts to the enrichment of the whole community. Each stage of the life cycle reminds us of the beauty that God is seeking in God's reign.

I was reminded of this at a recent baby shower in which two young parents were regaled with good wishes. As the couple received these blessings, a guest recounted the story of a recent trip to a small Asian village where the prevailing myth held that each baby was born with the precise gift needed by the village. Such a myth called upon the village to view each new child with expectation and respect for that child's emerging gift. The Christian story calls upon us similarly to resist the cultural impulse to devalue young people as incomplete adults or exploit them for purposes of the status quo. Instead, the Christian story of God manifesting beauty in the world calls us to expect more from youth and draw out their gifts, important for the human and created community to more closely resemble God's reign. Christian faith calls us to recognize young people as being energized by Christ for the healing of the world.

Youth as expressions of the beauty of God

God's love is not closed in upon itself, but the act of creation was an expression of love. Certainly, love that does not extend into the world beyond the narrow context of its awakening risks changing into something that is not love. Jürgen Moltmann, in *Theology of Play,* reveals that God created the world not of necessity, but as an expression of God's own creative freedom or play.[5] Creation is not simply a veil of tears from which we seek to escape or the neutral medium of our travail. In the playful and loving act of creation, God wove something of God's beauty into its very fabric. Moltmann extends an insight from Dutch biologist and philosopher F. J. J. Buytendijk to illustrate this playful beauty, "To put it simply, the birds are singing much more than Darwin permits." Nature serves not only the "preservation of individuals and species, but also displays its riches, and that is called freedom."[6] Nature is not bound to necessity alone but displays God's glory. Creation's playful rejoicing is what Buytendijk calls "the demonstrative value of being." Or, in Moltmann's view, its very being demonstrates God's playful nature.

All of creation bears the mark of God's beauty, and God speaks through human and created life. Young people in their developmental stage and social location bear marks of God's beauty and await the energizing of these for God's reign. If all of creation has beauty in excess of the necessities of evolution, can it also be that youth, as a stage of human life, represents something more than a transition to a normative adulthood — more than some developmental theorists would allow? Even as God is revealed in singing birds and the excesses of creation, so youth also reveal the beauty of God in the world — not simply when they fill our pews or rosters, or learn the churches doctrines, but as they embody their very youth. Youth, simply by virtue of being youth, offer some glimpse of God in excess of any economic utility or developmental norm of adulthood. As mentioned, the priority of commerce has shaped adolescent life in such a way as to obscure God's beauty revealed in young people.

The charism of youth for creating beauty

Although creation expresses something of God's beauty, we live in a broken world and need God to open these created gifts for participation in a greater beauty and fullness in God's reign. Life was created for right relationship with God and all of creation, yet the good purposes of creation are distorted when relationships are broken — when humans use each other and creation for their narrow purposes. The Holy Spirit among us is lovingly transforming broken relationships that prevent right relationship with God and each other. When we encounter the love and beauty of God, we are not only drawn close to God in love, but all of our powers can serve the holy work of love and beauty. Speaking of 1 Corinthians 7, in which Paul proclaims one calling and many people who are called, theologian Jürgen Moltmann observes, "When a person is called, whatever he [sic] is and brings with him [sic] becomes a charisma through his [sic] calling, since it is accepted by the Spirit and put at the service of the kingdom of God." Moltmann insists that Paul views the richness of our social location as potential charisma — whether male or female, Jew or Greek, young or old. All that we bring can be vitalized in the service of the reign of God. Moltmann quotes Ernst Käsemann, who suggests that "the lordship of Christ thrusts deeply into the secularity of the world."[7] "It is not merely special religious phenomena which become a charismatic experience for the believer.... It is the whole of bodily and social existence."[8] The Pauline idea of charisma brings the potential gift of youth into focus in a way that values them not as an incomplete version of adulthood, but as a gift to be energized for the reign of God — for creating a just and peaceful world in which human and created life can flourish into a beautiful whole. Youth in their beauty already reveal the holy in our midst and are potentially more fully in the service of the holy.

These theological ideas and biblical clues help us to focus on often forgotten dimensions of youth ministry. Youth are not merely to be exploited by marketers, ignored or diminished by theorists, demonized by police, or patronized by adults with a status quo in view. Embraced by congregations seeking God's reign, the energies of youth can become something different than in the domesticated contexts of adolescence in which they are restrained, placated, distracted, or channeled for a productive adulthood. Youth, by virtue of their social location, have unique perspectives and gifts that we are called to help mobilize for God's reign. Young people contribute beauty, energy, critical challenge, passion, compassion, curiosity, camaraderie, and many other gifts that invite us toward a reconciled world envisioned by the reign of God.

Hall's myth of adolescence revisited

How do the resources of Christian theology alter the myth of adolescence as a raging river that must be dammed up to prevent its dangerous and wasteful flow to the sea? Although deeply flawed, Hall's image of the river suggests alternate possibilities for imagining youth, when reformed by Christian theology. In the latter twentieth century, especially among industrial countries, we have learned much more about ecosystems than Hall had in view. In recent decades, we have discovered the importance of interrelated systems that nurture human life on this planet. If we see a river only in terms of its potential for industrial or recreational use, then we miss the intrinsic goodness and importance of the river itself. We miss the fact that beneath the river's surface there is a whole subterranean world teeming with life. There are fish, insects, algae, mysterious currents, warm and cold eddies, and whirlpools. We know that a tiny fish that seems unimportant may consume algae from the river bottom and may be a food source for larger fish. These tiny fish in themselves may not seem to have significant impact upon the river, but there are also other animals in proximity to the river that devour the larger fish that are fed by the tiny fish. And the algae, without the influence of the tiny fish, may overrun the river, consuming all the nutrients and oxygen in the water, thus denying life to other species. Further a dead river in which these tiny creatures have died greatly diminishes the quality of human life. We are learning that by viewing the river merely in terms of utility, as a source of hydroelectric energy or as a source of water, we risk a greater harm — the death of a river and the ecosystems that sustain it and us. Such harm outweighs the benefits of cheap electricity or water. Not only Christian theology with its beautiful vision of reconciliation, but also environmental science suggests that systems of natural life are intricate and interdependent.

In this century, our perspectives on youth have been dominated by expectation of their accommodation to existing political, economic, and social arrangements. Most contexts of contemporary youth emphasize their adaptation to the existing world, as members, students, observers, or consumers. Instead of damming the river of adolescence for any exploitative purpose or in support of the status quo, we are called to look to the life teeming in the river and its importance for the greater social good, human fullness, and the reign of God. To simply prepare youth for a promised future overlooks the importance of empowering youth to mobilize their gifts, including their prophetic gifts for engaging and healing this present world. Such empowerment does not exploit youth, but calls them to their best self, to embody their authentic role in the created family and the reign of God. To miss these gifts in favor of a utilitarian view of youth is also to ignore the relationship between the current myth of youth and the problems of the modern world. Like the undervalued and exploited river that becomes polluted, youth violence, depression, suicide, the failing system of education, fragmenting families, and increasingly apathetic and uninformed adults are directly related to how we currently warehouse our youth to await a productive adulthood. It is one thing for young people to endure a brief period of education and training for employment or as a rite of passage into adulthood. It is quite another to endure an ever longer period of limbo for a more questionable future.

Instead of asking how adolescence serves the status quo, we should reframe youth ministry to ask how young people as young people may serve human fullness, the created community, and the reign of God. And youth ministry should seek to cultivate the charisms glimpsed in their historical vocation — as agents of faith, justice, compassion, and human flourishing. It is one thing to understand youth ministry as means to ends — positively, educating youth in the stories of faith and instruction for baptism, or more negatively, keeping them contented while we seek our own lifestyles, or bolster our suffering "post-Christian" egos by adding them to our church rosters. It is an entirely different thing to value youth as youth with their unique vocation, to fully recognize the gifts that youth bring for human flourishing and the reign of God. While it may be entirely appropriate to invite youth to larger religious or civic purposes, it may also be faithful to honor youth in their vocation as youth. In this alternate theological vision, youth are not considered merely "adults in the making," but also as gifted with energy, beauty, creativity, compassion, idealism — not for warehousing, but for engaging the world now. Certainly this empowerment will require sponsoring and mentoring relationships with caring, experienced, faithful adults. But these adults, while protecting, caring for, and teaching the young, might also attend to the charisms of youth. The church has a responsibility to attend to the vocation of youth, helping them to fully embody the created glory of their youthfulness, to display God's glory in their gifts, and to use them for healing the world. The delightful irony is that when the gifts of young people flourish, human and created community is also strengthened. When youth's gifts are not respected and cultivated, the beauty of God is limited and the reign of God is postponed.

Youth do not make good monsters. They are too alive to the possibilities of human flourishing, to peace, justice, love, and vitality. This uneasy incongruity in which youth now find themselves does not easily allow for such life, but creates young people as the walking wounded. However, the swelling prisons, juvenile therapy centers, drug statistics, and the degradation of public schooling should be warning signs to us that young people can only be constrained to a point. Beyond a point, young people will refuse, resist, and react to these constraints. Youth ministry can no longer ignore its role in relation to these distortions, but must seek ways of engaging young people that encourage their gifts. We can no longer give an easy sound-bite gospel as a cure for a broken world. We must see the tears beneath the many masks of a monstrous adolescence and feel the compassion of God for these young ones. Only then can we begin considering ways to return youth to their best selves, to the purpose of their creation, to their vocation as youth. Only then can we open our communities to the beauty that God intends instead of the unnatural distortions created by commerce, ideology, or other purposes ignorant of youth or the Holy.

Notes

1. John Taylor Gatto, *The Underground History of American Education: A Schoolteacher's Intimate Investigation into the Problem of Modern Schooling* (New York: Oxford Village Press, 2002), 25.

2. Ibid.

3. James E. Côté and Anton L. Allahar, *Generation on Hold: Coming of Age in the Late Twentieth Century* (New York: New York University Press, 1996). These authors suggest that youth have become the new source of cheap labor for businesses that have capitalized on diminished status of youth and restructured the wage scale. There is an increased concentration of jobs at the bottom and upper-middle segments of wage distribution. There is a resulting decline in the wage base of young people — resulting from an increase in middle-age workers who consolidated their position in the upper middle class for whom the average wages rose 6 percent. The result is an increase in unemployment and poverty among youth. Since 1973 there has been a relative decrease in wages (declined 26 percent since 1973). Youth now on average earn less than 70 percent of what adult white males make, as opposed to 94 percent in 1967.

4. For details about this movement to criminalize adolescence see Mike Males, *Scapegoat Generation: America's War on Adolescents* (Monroe, Maine: Common Courage Press, 1996).

5. Jürgen Moltmann, ed., *Theology of Play,* trans. M. Douglas Meeks (New York: Harper and Row, 1972), 4ff.

6. Ibid.

7. Jürgen Moltmann, *The Spirit of Life: A Universal Affirmation* (Minneapolis: Fortress Press, 2003), 182.

8. Moltmann, *Theology of Play,* 4ff.

Two

Cultural forces and the crisis
in contemporary youth ministry

Although the memory of G. Stanley Hall has not endured, Hall's vision of adolescence as a river dammed and exploited accurately expresses the perspective that dominates the imagination of the North American church, distorting our relationships with youth and aggravating, if not creating, many of the problems in youth ministry. During the last 150 years, our social institutions have gradually removed young people from significant social roles in service to the common good or the reign of God and relegated them to passive roles as students, service workers, and consumers. But more significantly, our society in general and the church in particular have separated youth from their prophetic charism, and we are poorer because of it. Lacking historical perspective, the church has largely failed to understand this shift and instead has contributed to the domestication of young people.

In the previous chapter we explored a theological vision of adolescence. Yet, such visions of a more appreciative role for youth, however beautiful, do not suffice in themselves for transforming the "monster" of adolescence. We also need to assess the particular tensions of contemporary youth ministry, so that we can identify those "powers and principalities" or cultural forces that inhibit the charisms of youth and prevent adolescents from mobilizing as followers of Jesus. Only when we see these cultural inhibitions clearly can we hope to resist them. To this end, I suggest that we consider in more detail the multiple and often unacknowledged influences of culture on youth in general. From this vantage point, we then can turn to the perennial tensions of youth ministry in particular. I believe that we will find that the forces that distort the particular contexts of youth ministry stem from our normalized perception of youth, shaped by media, commerce, or distortions of developmental theorists — but rarely by our theological vision.

Culture and the heart of adolescence

Youth ministers are already familiar with the dangers of cultural assimilation. The prominent sexuality and vulgarity of media culture, for example, compose the subject of abundant cautionary lessons in typical youth ministry gatherings. Youth ministers continually try to protect young people from the influence of cultural messages that overtly conflict with Christian faith, such as song lyrics that extol atheism, drinking, or sexual promiscuity. However, culture entails more than song lyrics. It also includes the normalized patterned ways we organize our lives: our habits of commodity consumption, taking food, entertaining ourselves, driving automobiles, relating to work and leisure, our neighbors, the earth, and the strangers among us. These and other habits normalized in particular ways within our culture constitute a tacit curriculum that communicates powerful missives to adults and youth about what is appropriate and right. Many of the habits and relationships normalized by culture often embody values contrary to those of faith communities. Consequently, we sometimes imagine that if we could only replace secular culture with religious culture — or secular music with contemporary Christian music — we will have replaced a sinful message with a good or a holy one. Perhaps. But those who see only in this superficial manner engage the problem of culture on one level, and leave unexamined the cultural habits embedded in how we "use" commercial music, whether Christian or "secular," and the habits they encourage — habits of individualism, commodity consumption, sensationalism, celebrity worship, and passivity. All of these approaches to life profoundly contradict the gospel of Jesus, which advocates respect for others, contemplative consideration of self and God, thoughtful consideration of the world, and active confrontation of injustice.

Culture functions as a nearly invisible medium, in which we think and act — much as fish swim in water as their tacit environment without awareness of it. If we think of culture at all, we commonly regard its dangers as an ill wind rippling across the surface of an otherwise-still pond of adolescence. But in reality, culture in the context of our consumer society is much more pervasive than a breeze blowing across a surface: culture affects the waters of youth like an overgrowth of algae, which exhausts the oxygen in a pond and undermines the vitality of its ecosystems and its sustainability. Cultural pressures in the twenty-first century are not incidental to adolescence, pestering an otherwise healthy core structure. Rather, they reach into the very heart of adolescent life — destabilizing identity formation, manipulating desires, suppressing curiosity and comprehension of the world, determining status in peer groups, fragmenting family relationships, normalizing passivity, and inhibiting imagination of an alternate reign of God or a greater common good.

In the United States, "normal adolescence" includes expectations of habitual commodity and entertainment consumption, lukewarm consent to education as a credential (rarely as intrinsically valuable), ambition for wealth and status, sexual objectification of their own or others' bodies, alienation from adults and local sources of care and wisdom, marginalization from significant social roles, and ignorance of economic or political structures. Of course, not all youth fall into these patterns or participate in them to the same degree, but those who resist full participation in these cultural norms, values, and beliefs increasingly find themselves deemed odd by peers and adults alike. Pressure to conform to these expectations is only one aspect of contemporary culture, which distorts the structures of adolescent life and allows little more than a domesticated[1] or passive form of Christian discipleship.

While Christian faith has always contended with the dangers of culture — whether Roman, Stalinist, or consumerist — rarely have

distorted cultural forces so subtly pervaded human life and contra-
dicted Christian faith as they do today. The entertainment media
serves as our most visible culprit for promoting messages and habits
that conflict with the gospel, but other adolescent cultural institutions also contribute. One such institution is the contemporary high
school. While offering young people opportunities for learning and
relating, high schools also inculcate youth with negative values —
of *competition* for grades, status, and jobs; of *utility*, or the appreciation of things for how they can be used or exploited instead of
for their intrinsic goodness (the utility of learning is seen as a credential for a future job; people are seen in terms of their utility as
barriers to success; jobs are assessed solely in terms of financial re-
ward, not how they invite the reign of God); of *conformity* to fashion
and popular norms; and of *coolness*, or the suppression of passion
and compassion in favor of market-imposed desires or the mercu-
rial shifts of homogeneous peer-group norms. These institutions and
the values they promote by abstracting youth from the natural and
the political world and intergenerational communities invite a diminished regard for adults, the earth, local communities, and youth's
own signature gifts. High schools prevent young people from learning
how intergenerational communities solve real problems, relegating
youth to age-homogeneous contexts where formal learning remains
disconnected from their curiosity and concerns and from their local
communities.

When we accept media consumption and the high school (in its
most prominent version) as normal or "natural" outlets for adolescents, we unwittingly accept powerful — and potentially damaging —
messages about the appropriate social roles of young people. Historically, youth have formed healthy identities by participating in
meaningful work, in a range of social relationships, and in the traditions of the community. Today, however, youth must achieve identity
amid manipulations by commercial culture and the fluid peer culture of high school. Participation in these institutions of adolescence
might seem harmless enough or even a bit "romantic": we adults
often remember our high school days with some nostalgia. Yet these

institutions form youth in ways that help determine our perception of American adolescence as passive, irresponsible, selfish, or danger-ous — while youth, however reluctantly, live into our expectations for them. Churches that view the gospel of Jesus as involving bold participation with God's healing of the world today find their mission little supported by other spheres of adolescent life — neither in peer relationships, nor in schools, nor even in entertainment. Contempo-rary culture, especially as shaped by our market economy, influences adolescents, colonizing their values, norms, habits, and imaginations. Such a thorough colonization of adolescent thought and habit is unique in history and makes the gospel — as it was meant to be lived — sound like an implausible fairy tale at least for some youth.

The myth of the dam that G. Stanley Hall constructed to prevent "precocity" or to limit the social activity of youth has echoed in var-ious ways throughout numerous cultural spheres, including political structures that prevent greater participation of youth and various laws that criminalize experimental behavior. Many communities con-tinually reject school bond issues and adjustments in the minimum wage, while supporting entertainment media and high schools that keep young people passive. The culture is invested in a developmen-tal understanding that defines adolescence as a "moratorium,"[2] and a job market that defines adolescence as a time of training for future employment or as a time to exploit low-skilled, low-paid employees. The culture is filled with exploitative media images of dangerous, ir-responsible, or incapable youth that make adults fearful of inviting them to be full partners.

Although few know of Hall's theory, its logic has proliferated, with great impact on youth and our society. Just as exploitation and pollution distort the natural environment by creating an unhealthy ecosystem unable to support life, so our domesticating versions of adolescence distort youth themselves, rendering young people apa-thetic, low in self-esteem, unstable in identity, and prone to violence or alienation. But the impact of this distorted adolescence — alien-ated from their God-breathed charisms as agents of change — is not limited to individual teens. Its toxicity spills over into schools, neighborhoods, families, and congregations, threatening their institutions and society in general. In the same manner as the river that cannot be exploited forever without degrading the surrounding ecosystem, ignoring the gifts of youth is culminating in a crisis in the human systems that surround youth — families, schools, and communities.

This "degradation of the environment of youth" takes particular forms in congregations in ministry with youth. Making matters worse is the church's unwitting complicity in the domestication of young people, a problem that becomes clear when we reflect on the practical struggles of youth ministry. How might we best go about this kind of reflection? Because the domestication of youth has its origins in a pervasive cultural system, investigating discrete situations or isolated examples may not be the best way to explore how cultural pressures affect youth discipleship. We can obtain a better grasp of the systemic nature of the problem when we view its manifestations in "clusters." Put differently, viewing the "parts" in relation to the "whole" allows us to glimpse how youth ministry itself remains embedded in a complex *system* of adolescence. In what follows, I (1) make some introductory remarks about my own reasons for addressing the struggles of youth ministry; (2) identify several core tensions of youth ministry that impede formation of youth as disciples; and (3) drawing from my analysis of these tensions, I make some preliminary suggestions for alternate strategies or directions for youth ministry.

My story

I write about alternate approaches to youth ministry not simply because I am intellectually curious, but primarily because of the tensions that have pervaded my own twenty-three years of youth ministry in various parts of the United States: Mississippi, Kentucky, Alaska, California, and Georgia. I do not mean to claim that the tensions I experienced are universal. At the same time, I have observed them consistently in my own and other youth ministers' work over many years in numerous ecclesial settings. My observations remain informal in that I have not here conducted a statistical analysis. Yet by the same token, they are not casual observations. I take them seriously in no small part because the tensions between culture and youth ministry constitute a significant daily struggle for me as a youth minister, never drifting far from my attention. The themes that I elaborate below have also emerged in various forms in conversations with youth ministers from across the nation — those whom I have taught or with whom I have consulted.

As a youth minister, I spent many years and countless sleepless nights trying, with only partial or temporary success, to fashion creative responses to these recurring problems. Only after much time did I begin to recognize the cultural system of adolescence, of which the particular tensions I was facing in my ministry with youth were but manifestations. Biological or psychological developmental theories of adolescence cannot fully account for these conflicts. Nor can we explain them as failed strategies of particular congregations or youth ministers. At bottom, the perennial tensions of youth ministry point suspiciously to the social construction of adolescence, the "elephant in the living room," the rarely discussed fixture of youth ministry around which our work with youth seeks to quietly tiptoe, avoiding any challenge to its status quo.

What difference does it make to acknowledge the elephant — that is, to concede that the problems of youth ministry stem from deeply entrenched cultural structures of adolescence, and not just from the myriad of epiphenomenal conflicts that youth ministers must confront? To continue status quo youth ministry, however vigorously, without reflecting on the larger structures that undergird it, is akin to rearranging the deck chairs on the *Titanic*. We cannot resolve these ubiquitous tensions simply by applying a little more effort or a few more resources, as many youth ministers assume. Instead, we need to focus *critically* and *creatively* on the nature, structure, and function of these cultural barriers to forming youth as disciples of Jesus. In what follows, I will make clearer these cultural constructions, especially as they relate to youth ministry.

Core tensions of youth ministry

Not surprisingly, many of us have failed to recognize contemporary youth ministry as being in crisis: our inability to see it as a problem is a sign of its normalization. The crisis has continued for so long that many now view the problem as "just the way things are in youth ministry." Further, the average tenure for youth ministers in a congregation remains dismally short, around eighteen months: not many stay in one particular church long enough to understand the root problems of youth ministry, including those that culminate in youth ministers' leave taking. To gain an introductory sense of this crisis, I invite you as readers to suspend those ideas about youth ministry that would construe the following concerns as "normal" or "natural." I invite you, in short, to view them through the eyes of someone from another culture or era, or perhaps through the eyes of God.

Youth are distracted by the demands of success

In North America, contemporary adolescence functions largely as a preparatory stage of educational training for a future as an employee. While youth certainly entertain other pursuits — such as romance, friendship, sports, religion, or even intellectual curiosity — most adults and youth view these pursuits as secondary to the primary goal of education, which is to get a good job. Among the predominant cultural myths is that education is necessary to ensure a good job as an adult. While the specifics of this myth have shifted somewhat in recent decades to include, not only the necessity of a high school diploma, but also undergraduate and graduate education, virtually every child in North America grows up with this expectation. Education, particularly for the middle class, is a fundamental aspect of adolescent life in America — fraught with fear and promise.

While education is important for a number of reasons, too often it functions purely to prepare youth for individual security, status, and wealth; and it consequently obscures other ways that we as Christians may wish to form our young people. Especially in uncertain economic climates, we focus on their security at the expense of their flourishing.

By "flourishing," I mean here, among other things, helping youth to cultivate their signature strengths and gifts, their responsibilities in a human and natural community, and their formation in an alternative story that calls them to participate in God's reign. Youth and families' nearly exclusive focus on preparation for a secure future presents severe limits for youth ministry that seeks to foster faithful flourishing. Church or youth group almost invariably takes a backseat whenever school or work pressures demand young people's attention. Consider the following statements familiar to most youth ministers:

- "My child will not be attending youth group this semester because her grades are slipping below what she needs to get into a good college."

- "I can't come to the spiritual life retreat this weekend. My science project is due next week."

- "I have homework tonight and can't join the youth group serving food at the homeless shelter."

- "I am sensing that God may be leading me to work with the poor, but my mom and dad have told me since I was two years old that I would be a doctor. What do I do?"

- "Pastor, why must you engage our youth in contemplative prayer or discuss such weird things as consumerism and social justice? Why can't you just teach them manners and morals to equip them for a normal life?"

Families that support, encourage, and even coerce youth to pursue culturally defined success exert tremendous negative pressure on the religious formation of youth. Confronting youth (and families) who are distracted by the demands of success is difficult, given that many of the priorities represented above — education, good work, and responsibility — may be seen as virtues and appropriately championed by youth ministers. This threat to Christian faith becomes all the more difficult to confront because it comes not in the form of stereotypical terrorists, Hollywood elites, or other perceptible forms of evil with fangs dripping, but instead as loving parents who care deeply about their children. Regardless of the source, when the core values of our congregations shift from love of God and neighbor to love or desire for something else — security, status, or wealth — it becomes difficult to avoid the recognition that we have traveled beyond a Christian religious perspective.

In *Black and White Styles of Youth Ministry,* William Myers clarifies the problem with middle-class versions of success when he discusses the clash of material and religious interests in one white suburban congregation. Consider these verbatim quotes from the youth minister of one congregation:

> When you talk about ultimates here...ultimates are the education. Ultimates are success socially....Two years ago one of the first retreats occurred where I started really looking at discipleship. I did a process where we experienced what binds us in our lives with ropes, literally tying us in knots, with me ultimately cutting off each rope with a knife, "in the name of Jesus Christ...." But I heard so much flack from parents who said, "What did you do out there?" You know, "What did you do to those kids...?"[3]

This youth minister presided over a clash of cultures in which the parents feared Christian ideas that might lead their children to question or reject the dominant or normative track of success. From the parents' viewpoint, anything that might conflict with the commitment to education or career preparation was automatically suspect.

This success orientation affects youth in particular ways. For example, this same youth minister also sponsored "eye-openers," or visits to the nearby city aimed at introducing youth to the struggles of the poor. Rather than igniting young people's sense of compassion, however, the experience had an opposite effect. Myers tells of one young woman who delivered a frank response.

> [She realized] that she had a good life now and also realized that she would have a hard time maintaining that lifestyle.... She also realized that it was a stressful pursuit but didn't know any

better direction and also didn't have confidence that she could attain such an economic level for herself. She was in a double bind. If anything the "eye-opener" showed her why she had to stay on the ladder. If she didn't achieve success, go to college, continue to compete, she would "fall off the ladder" and be lost — wind up like those people she saw in the city.[4]

According to Myers, this young woman ultimately quit the youth group in order to focus on getting into a good college. In the Gospels, being introduced to the poor functions as an opportunity to meet the Christ ("Lord, when did we see you?"). In relation to the cultural system of success that young people inevitably internalize to one degree or another, however, exposure to the poor can become a threat to security, even prompting, as in the case above, a frenetic retreat into the security of the middle class.

The point I want to make here is not that middle-class aspirations always contradict the gospel of Jesus. Clearly they do not, as can be seen, for example, in the middle class's invention of civil society.[5] But unless we view youth ministry as a place to reflect critically and theologically on the aspirations of class and as a place to cultivate alternate conceptions of vocation, we will likely end up with a vastly diluted faith that serves the whims of culture and class. We risk allowing our faith to be co-opted by our lifestyles and shaped by forces as diverse as consumerism, political ideologies, nationalism, ethnic traditions, or market values. When the church fails to teach youth to grasp the integrity of the gospel and alternate ways of living faithfully or to provide practical skills for discerning these alternatives, we essentially relegate the gospel to tacit support of the cultural status quo. And as many of our young people conclude, "If that is all there is to the Christian faith, then why bother?"

When Jesus commanded us to love God and neighbor, he did not intend his injunction as a mere supplement to an otherwise unreflective middle-class life (or to any other class or identity that contradicts God's intentions of love), merely "stapled onto the edge," so to speak. Instead, he saw God-love and neighbor-love centers that shape all of life's values and activities. Young people require critical and imaginative skills and congregational support for discovering vocations more open to this radical call for love of God and neighbor. If we relegate youth ministry to the position of support mechanism for pursuit of culturally defined success, how can we possibly encourage them to take seriously the "scandal" of the gospel that challenges the cultural status quo? If the church limits its teaching efforts to helping youth advance their material success, then those commitments important for full human flourishing and for the reign of God remain unfulfilled.

An exclusive focus on preparing youth for an ideal adult future not only condemns Jesus's great command to love to marginal status, but also minimizes the value of youth *as* youth. When culture normalizes adolescence as a preparatory stage of life, it disconnects young people from responsibilities within their own community and from their resources for healing their community. Young people are left dreaming about the individualistic promises of "goodies of life," not the good life. Quite simply, adolescence has become a "dream state" of American life, or a state that looks ever forward to an ideal future. The dreamy optimism of adolescence has become a virtual cliché when we think about American teens. But how could it be otherwise, given that we so rarely allow our youth to explore the world beyond the high school or their headphones — or the church basement?

Youth are marginalized by the faith community

The myth that adolescence is simply a preparatory stage of life funds the high school and involves it with preparing teens for individual material success, but often fails to cultivate young people's range of gifts.[6] Those few gifts that are cultivated usually remain confined to the artificial world of high school. We have, quite simply, marginalized youth from meaningful activity. Consider the following scenes drawn from representative congregations.

- While the administrative council is struggling earnestly with how best to embody the gospel in outreach to the church's neighborhood, young people are playing volleyball in the courtyard.

- While adults are engaging in orderly worship in the recently re-modeled sanctuary before prominent television cameras, youth gather in the gym for "youth worship" — consisting of silly choruses, simplistic object lessons, and games to keep their attention.

- While adults join in the parlor with the professor from the local seminary, to explore biblical themes of justice, the youth group is having a pizza social.

- During regular church potluck lunches, youth habitually sit on one side of the fellowship hall while adults sit on the other.

These examples drawn from existing congregations point to a systemic problem: many congregations limit youth involvement in church activities to token participation. Rarely do we invite youth to participate in the liturgy or the planning and implementation of church ministries. And on those few occasions when we do invite them, we find it tempting to patronize their efforts.

More often than not, youth are simply relegated to the church attic or basement to play games or otherwise engage in frivolous activities. Congregations that dismiss youth in this way simply perpetuate cultural assumptions about young people's supposed inabilities and questionable value. These cultural assumptions stem in part from media portrayals of youth as violent, irreverent, irresponsible, or incapable; the assumptions take on added potency when we factor in the genuine exhaustion of adults themselves, whose own lifestyle distractions from responsibilities of faith make youth mentoring seem an insurmountable chore.

Whatever the precise cause, when congregations marginalize teens they ignore the enormous contributions that young people have made for centuries in their civic and faith communities — for example, in the civil rights movement of the 1960s, the environmental movement, the peace movements of the last two centuries, and the major revivals of modern and ancient history (some think Jesus's disciples themselves were teenagers). In fact, in preindustrial America, teens commonly worked alongside older folks and earned adult responsibility and respect by age fifteen or sixteen. Youth today spend their time in institutions nearly devoid of formal adult sponsorship or mentorship. Contemporary young people negotiate their personal ethics, habits, values, and vocational decisions in virtual isolation from adults. Those adults who work with youth often function as distant administrators, but rarely as practical mentors.

The fears that prompt congregations to restrict the roles of young people have their cause not in how youth really are, but in the cultural domestication of young people and their systematic abstraction from positions of real responsibility and practical experience. Sometimes we justify segregating young people by suggesting that youth have their own cognitive and emotional requirements. While teens do possess a distinct configuration of age-appropriate qualities and needs, a deeper reading of developmental theory reveals that normal development actually depends on the *integration* of youth into intergenerational communities and their exploring relationships beyond family and peers. Encounters with persons and situations outside a young person's familiar territory enhance the adolescent task both of achieving formal operations (as prescribed in cognitive theory) and of learning about mutual perspective-taking (as discussed in moral theory).

In addition, while adolescence certainly represents a unique stage of cognitive, moral, and faith development that makes a young person's way of knowing and being qualitatively different from adults, in the best of circumstances these differences do not disqualify youth from leadership but actually qualify them for distinctive forms of prophetic leadership that the church needs. In consequence, we must not simply write off the idealism of youth as a perspective inferior to that of adults. Youthful idealism can remind adults of ideals that we ourselves have long since compromised or abandoned under social pressures — in much the way that the Hebrew prophets reminded the culturally assimilated Israelites of the forgotten justice demanded by the Torah. In short, if we truly consider as spiritual gifts the signature strengths of youth, we find ourselves called not to isolate them, but to cultivate them for God's reign and the common good symbolized therein.

Youth are detached from the material conditions of the community

A third cultural problem challenging youth ministry is the detachment of young people from the material conditions — including economic, social, and political — of their communities. Today's youth grow up within an artificial high school or "youth culture" dominated by entertainment, ceaseless peer camaraderie, and interminable preparation for a distant future. Isolation within these contexts physically and emotionally removes young people from their communities and from personal experiences by which to grasp public issues such as poverty, HIV-AIDS, public health, or war and violence, in which their natural curiosity might encourage a greater understanding of how the world is constructed. Instead, young people pass their time in classroom learning environments that are abstracted from experiences of the wounds and blessings of the world. In turn, alienated forms of learning that predominate in many high schools shape a resistance to learning in general that spills over into the church. Consider the following observations of teachers and youth ministers:

- Many young people know only the most basic facts about community, state, federal, or global governance. Yet many can name the major movies and top recordings of the past year.

- Many young people know little about their family's finances. They also fail to grasp the complexities of the job base in their area and the role of corporations, governments, and citizens in shaping their communities.

- Many youth cannot identify the fifty American states or the nations of the world. Issues surrounding war, ethnic conflicts, globalization, and labor battles remain beyond many young people's grasp.

Along with other educators, I insist that such ignorance, or intelligence focused on trivialities, does not reflect so much the inability of youth as their social location that relegates them to isolated homogenous groups apart from experiences of other people's suffering. Indeed, youth of earlier times displayed no lack of ability. As we saw earlier, youth of preindustrial America and Europe once held significant social roles within communities in support of the common good. These social roles required young people to understand their community's history, organization, and problems, and to envision solutions for its betterment. Education was not only accomplished in formal settings of school, but largely came in the struggle to be a responsible member of a community. Youth in medieval villages once gathered at May Day, Mid-Summer's Festival, Guy Fawkes Night, the Feast of Fools, and other celebrations for eating, drinking, singing, dancing, and gaming. Commonly these youth gatherings evolved into challenges to the corrupt status quo that included burning effigies of offenders, singing bawdy songs, marking stigmas on door frames, marching for higher wages and lower bread prices, and generally seeking a more just equilibrium for their communities. While in former times these energies of youth found expression in seeking the common good, we in the latter half of the twentieth and early twenty-first centuries have nearly succeeded in stilling their political voices. Today's youth know little about what their parents do for a living, or how they make decisions, create budgets, or make spending decisions. They know far less about how their local communities are governed. Even less do they understand the social causes of poverty, including the recession of the industrial base, competition with foreign labor markets, white flight to the suburbs, or the depletion of urban resources.

The abstraction of youth from these material conditions of their communities affects the sphere of youth ministry in subtle ways. At its best, youth ministry helps youth cultivate a faith that leads naturally back into the world — to seek justice, care for the earth, show hospitality to strangers, and generally respond wherever they perceive God's call. Yet in much contemporary youth ministry, faith constitutes an abstraction; it has relevance as a private benefit or for a heavenly realm far more than for the material conditions of this world. This abstracted faith removes youth from consideration of the concrete world in which they and their families live and work, and in which some are exploited and suffer.

It is difficult to engage youth in theological reflection

High schools are not the only institution to abstract youth from concrete experiences and understandings of their communities. The commercial youth culture industry contributes to this abstraction by connecting youth to "youth culture," rather than to local communities, homes, churches, and neighborhoods. With the recession of adult influence and local authority from adolescent lives, the entertainment media now form most of our youth's sensibilities, obscuring the religious significance of issues like consumption, sexual objectification, or violence. It is difficult to overstate the extent to which media manipulates the desires and distorts the relationships of youth. As expressed by Bob Pittman, the founder of MTV, "We don't shoot for the 14-year-olds, we own them."[7]

This colonization affects young people in ways that inhibit youth ministry. Not only have contemporary adolescents become largely inured or numb to a buzzing mass of media images, but this electronic environment also diminishes their ability to think critically and imaginatively about the world. The problem carries over quickly into the youth ministry setting. If television programmers have given up, as they have, on complex plots because they know that youth with remote controls are likely to change the channel in the absence of an immediately gratifying or stimulating program that includes sex or violence, then youth ministers might also recognize young people's similar aversion to complexity at church. Media consumption promotes the value of things over people, superficiality over depth, objectification over otherness, utility over relationship, individualism over interrelationship, sensation over understanding, and passivity over activity. These conditions in turn make it increasingly difficult for youth ministers to engage young people's intellects as a means of loving God and neighbor. Consider the following complaints and comments often heard by youth ministers:

- "We study all week long at school. Why do we have to study here at church too?"
- "I don't care what scholars and theologians say. The world is too complicated. I'm just going to love Jesus, and I will be okay."
- "I know that youth in my church don't understand the history of Israel or the cultural context of early Christianity, but they have committed their hearts to Jesus."
- "I love youth group when we have rock bands, but I can't stand it when we have Bible study."

Many youth ministers report that their teens seem unable to grasp complicated ideas or attend to anything that is not sheer distraction, entertainment, or easily consumed — amounting to a sort of mass attention deficit disorder. A recent PBS *Frontline* special, "Merchants of Cool," illuminated the methods of the entertainment industry in seducing our youth.[8] Entertainment corporations spend billions of dollars each year to learn more effective ways of "hooking" our young people so that they will buy more products and identify with particular items and brands. Advertising agencies boast of their conquest of the "Mooks," or young men who have grown up watching professional wrestling and action/adventure movies on television. These young men have become addicted to the thrill of action and violence, and the entertainment industry is only too happy to support their habit. Similarly, the PBS report identified the phenomenon of the "Midriffs," or young women who, like their role model Britney Spears, have learned that exploiting their sexuality provides a form of social power. Analyzing the world critically and theologically lies well beyond the comfort zones — but not the capability — of many young people. Among other things, critical reflection would call into question the utility of their wholesale consumption of media, an activity that youth depend on for forming contemporary peer relationships and signifying their own status. Too often, the extent to which a young person participates in and "buys into" popular culture determines his or her status among peers.

While youth seem outwardly comfortable with such distortions of human life, they risk never finding authentic selfhood or Christian vocation described by Jesus as love of God, neighbor, and self. Youth who cannot engage their faith in critical relation to culture risk either abandoning their faith entirely or splitting it off as a separate aspect of their middle-class (or otherwise status quo) life. Such a separated faith does not threaten youth or youth culture; indeed, it remains so domesticated as to hardly distinguish their lives from persons outside the church. Is this really the kind of faith we want our youth to cultivate? Despite a current anti-intellectual trend in American Christianity, the marks of a Christian disciple surely should include understanding the world in which we live and the God who moves us to respond to this world. To fully embody love of God and neighbor, youth need skills for investigating the structures of contemporary life and the causes of human distortion, including their own exploitation by the entertainment and fashion industries, together with the conditions that push youth of developing countries into sweatshops to produce American fashion products.

My point here is not to demonize popular culture in wholesale fashion. It is simply to suggest that youth ministry cannot afford simply to baptize popular culture by packaging Christian content in fashionable styles. Popular culture does more than sneak some bad language in through the back door. It forms the norms, values, beliefs, and habits of our youth, not just through its content but also through its form: sensationalism, individualism, and rampant consumption. These cultural forms cannot embody Christian virtues of patience and self-control, nor can they teach us the practices of contemplation and seeking justice. Instead, they merely convey to us a story about what corporate culture finds to be appropriate, good, and worthwhile as we expend our resources. This "story" amounts to a spirituality of consumption. It runs counter to the gospel, regardless of the content of isolated television shows with countercultural messages. For this reason, youth ministry *must* engage young people in the rigorous use of their minds to "test the spirits" of culture.

Critical skills alone, however, remain insufficient to spark the imaginations of young people for participation in God's reign. If Christian faith is to resist rather than affirm a culture of individualism and consumption, young people need to be confronted with the logic of their faith in ways that inspire new, joyful, and just models of reality, models that include young people's participation with God in the reconciliation of the world. The Christian story helps us in this effort: it naturally resists the packaging of popular culture and, it fosters its own perspectives and practices. Such perspectives call us to imagine and create a better world in which all creatures flourish in respectful and peaceful interrelationship.

Youth ministers face a great temptation to mirror popular culture, and in doing so, to accommodate the gospel for easy consumption. We tend to organize activities around sound-bite lessons and sensationalism, because young people respond to such strategies. The temptation is only intensified by the popular practice of assessing youth ministry's "successes" according to numbers. But in the long run, framing Christian faith as culturally acceptable risks setting up our young people for viewing their faith as superfluous or minimizing its power to transform. Youth ministers thus face the daunting task of helping shape alternative images of God's reign that function not merely as minor adjustments to popular culture but as distinctive alternatives. These alternatives should help youth orient their lives around the Christian story with its radical challenge: "Thy will be done, on earth as it is in heaven."

The isolation, burnout, and turnover of youth ministers

The ongoing crisis of youth ministry takes on additional difficulties when we consider the problem of continuity in adult leadership. Disturbingly, the average tenure of a youth minister with a congregation is very brief.[9] Anyone who has struggled to understand the state of youth ministry encounters a variety of reasons for the burnout and turnover of youth ministers.

- Many suspect the low pay of youth ministers: "Why should the congregation pay more for glorified baby-sitting?"

- Others point to the lack of congregational support, including funding and volunteers: "Who has the time? I've got a full-time job taking care of my own family."

- The isolation of youth ministry from the rest of congregational life results in alienation that ranges from the youth minister's development of entirely different theological frameworks at odds with those of the congregation, to general lack of trust in the youth minister and his or her youth: "Who knows what's going on down in that basement? What's she teaching those kids?"

While these factors certainly contribute to the isolation and burnout of youth ministers, I suggest we view them as part of a broader system that constrains youth ministers.

To better understand this system, recall the different ways in which we have identified "youth culture" as the main force behind the distractions of youth, inhibiting their embodiment of Christian faith and constituting a key barrier to effective youth ministry. Many youth ministers assume, in turn, that youth culture is a given or an unassailable reality of adolescent life, and further, that the gospel must necessarily be proclaimed in the same popular idiom. Youth ministers often view their role as one of "cultural detective" or "spy": we must infiltrate the secret ranks of youth culture in order to locate an easily accessible way for teaching youth the gospel. Moreover, we must do so without actually challenging youth culture itself. Congregations expect youth ministers to be young, "cool," "hip," and experts in youth culture. Church leaders and parents urge their youth ministers to immerse themselves in popular culture in order to learn a language by which to express the gospel in culturally relevant forms. Youth ministers, in turn, dutifully search for cultural hooks upon which to hang our message, to show youth that we respect them and their culture.

Finding such cultural hooks, however, remains more difficult than it first appears. Youth-exploiting corporations such as MTV employ hordes of researchers to detect any slight shift among youthful trendsetters in order to shape their programming accordingly. Corporations capture advanced expressions of cool, turn them into products, and mass-market them to all teens until their market potential is saturated. The product disappears, and the process begins again. These engines of commerce have succeeded in prompting youth culture to make significant shifts every six months.[10] Now if identifying and marketing these constantly metamorphosing expressions of youth remains difficult for well-funded, well-staffed corporations, how much more difficult is the same task going to be for a lone youth minister? Sadly, we have a situation in which it is no longer sufficient for youth ministers to understand and live the gospel and invite youth alongside us. We must now find marketing hooks to make the gospel appealing. In short, youth ministers find themselves at odds not only with the unreflective assumptions of parents about cultural versions of success, but also with youth whose sensibilities about what is cool are constantly manipulated by the youth culture industry.

Youth ministry that seeks validity solely from youth's attachment to culture lacks a fundamental trust in the goodness and beauty of God. I do not wish to oversimplify the complex relationship of the gospel to culture. After all, Jesus utilized agricultural metaphors from his own culture to describe the reign of God. His use of such metaphors reminds us that we cannot — and need not — simply escape the conceptual fields of our cultural milieu. But Jesus never utilized his culture in order to make his message easily consumable or unchallenging. The opposite was actually the case. Contemporary youth ministers must ask how youth ministry functions in relation both to popular culture and the challenge of the gospel.

While some churches can afford to dedicate substantial financial resources to entertaining their youth, small and mid-sized churches often exhaust themselves trying to do the same. I encourage us to consider, instead, those congregations that have learned to invite young people alongside adults, not to seek entertainment, but to participate in traditional practices of faith that engage young people on all levels. Congregations that encourage youth to use their hearts, minds, souls, and strength in the world around them do not experience any lack of energy. This kind of ministry generates its own energy — or, more accurately, it draws from God's spirit. Adults and youth who together follow Christ into the world rarely lack for motivation. They gain the vitality and energy that arises as they connect to something larger than consumption — namely, God's movement in the world. Youth ministry cannot empower youth for faith in abstraction, but only in the activity of being faithful. Faith flourishes in acts of reconciliation, in active love of God and neighbor. If I hear youth ministers rightly, many are reporting that this kind of youth ministry, though demanding, constantly renews body, mind, and spirit.

Clues for transforming youth ministry

The tension between the gospel and the cultural limitations of adolescent life constitutes a crisis at the core of contemporary youth ministry. Encouraging young people to embody Christian faith within the boundaries of "normal" adolescence is like trying to grow an oak tree in an orange crate. Either the tree will burst the confines of the crate or the resulting plant will become severely dwarfed and malformed by what surrounds it. Being a normal teenager precludes many of the most significant ways of being faithful. Teenage life does not naturally conduce to practices of simplicity, contemplation, discernment, seeking justice, or love of God and neighbor.

If the constraints of normal adolescence inhibit the faithfulness of youth, much like a crate limits the growth of a young oak, then it is a mistake to assume that an oak tree grown for years within an orange crate can grow to its full size once the crate is removed. The limitations of adolescence, a "life stage" now lasting for a longer time period than ever before in history, become engrained habits that continue beyond the teen years and limit the embodiment of adult Christian vocation. This added threat of the domestication of *adult* faith ought to broaden the conversation well beyond those of us with an immediate interest in youth ministry. Entire congregations need to explore forces that inhibit faith among young people *and* adults.

To extend the metaphor of the crate, imagine the frustration of the gardener charged with the responsibility of cultivating the confined oak trees. For decades youth ministers have attempted to cultivate Christian discipleship within the constraints of American adolescence. Faced with such daunting limitations, however, youth ministers have quickly found that more intelligence, resources, or hard work improve their ministry only in minor ways. Youth do not need more activity or more entertainment; they need ministers who dedicate whatever resources they already have to understanding and resisting the distortions of culture and living into the way of Jesus — and helping youth to do the same.

G. Stanley Hall's vision of adolescence, which Hall described as analogous to a river, prescribed the role of teachers and youth workers as creators of dams for channeling the energies of youth so as to advance industrial progress. Hall valued the gifts of youth — their golden energy, romance, adventure, camaraderie, curiosity, and compassion — but he sensed great risk in allowing these gifts to enter the world unchecked or unregulated. The fundamental contradiction of Hall's doctrine, then, lies in the mistaken assumption that we can simultaneously honor the gifts of youth or allow those gifts to flourish *and* exploit youth for our own purposes, whether nationalism, commercial interests, preservation of the status quo, padding church roll numbers, or some other purpose that renders youth a means and not an end. Whether we relegate youth to factories, as in the beginning of the twentieth century, or assign them to never-ending classrooms, as we do today, we fundamentally distort and obscure their prophetic gifts of idealism, creativity, and compassion. When we exile our youth to commercial culture and to institutions that support culture, we prevent them from service to the reign of God with its concern for the common good.

Hall's vision of adolescence is not our only option for theorizing youth. If we mine the resources of Christian theology, as I suggested in chapter 1, we find that youth possess unique gifts. Cultivating these gifts contributes to the reign of God and the common good envisioned therein. But when cultural, political, and social forces ignore or suppress these gifts, hoping to utilize only those parts of youthful energy that can be readily exploited, we risk not only the loss of a redemptive movement of God among our youth, but also the broader pollution of our entire common life.

This chapter has elaborated some of the manifestations in youth ministry of this toxic version of adolescence. I have argued that this "toxic adolescence" binds youth to a "youth culture" disconnected from their communities, or from the wisdom of elders and an awareness of conditions that might challenge and expand faith. This troubled version of adolescence further removes young people from the centers of congregational and communal life, dispatching them to the margins where they play games and take part in socials. And it renders problematic our efforts to invite and form youth as followers of Christ, leaving many of us in youth ministry exhausted and burned out as a result. Clearly, this chapter has not exhausted all the points of tension in youth ministry. When viewed critically, however, the tensions we have mentioned point to deep structural problems at the heart of the institution of adolescence.

How might these components of adolescent life — church, education, entertainment — be different if, for example, we valued youth not only for their future potential, but also for present gifts? How might adolescence look if we refused to exile youth from contexts of social responsibility? How might adolescent life be different if youth education entailed not just job training, but also exploring the world through active experiments that engaged faith with physical, political, and social problems and did so in ways responsive to young people's innate curiosity and questions? And how might adolescence look different if we did not isolate our youth in peer groups but held serious expectations that teens should be integrated into an intergenerational community?

If youth ministry is to break out of its cultural captivity, we must frame our work in a different way. We need, in short, a new paradigm of youth ministry. Such a paradigm should challenge the distortions of youth culture and the domesticated institution of adolescence by introducing a range of practices integral to Christian faith and life: for example, prayer, worship, reading and interpreting scripture, hospitality to strangers, seeking justice, creativity, care of the earth, Sabbath keeping, feasting, and more.[11] These practices shape young and old in ways that run counter to culture, providing a means of resisting cultural colonization. While an ecology of practices such as these remains important for youth ministry and congregational life, we must take care not simply to add new practices onto an otherwise unreflective life. Instead, we should encourage the gradual refinement and transformation of adolescent life through discernment. In this book I am arguing for a youth ministry framed by the practice of discernment. Such an approach to youth ministry has the following aims:

- To help young people assess the cultural norms that promote certain images of success and ignore others.

- To help young people attend to and cultivate their gifts that push beyond the margins of the congregation into their appropriate role in God's reign.

- To help young people connect their stories to God's story that sometimes confirms and sometimes criticizes culture.

- To help young people use the fullness of their abilities — hearts, minds, souls, and strength — in their faith journey.

- To resist the influence of culture that inhibits their search for ways of loving God and neighbor.

- To engage congregations and youth ministers in naming and resisting the forces of culture that prevent fullness of Christian discipleship. This includes helping youth ministers seek appropriate ways of relating to youth culture — appreciation and critique.

- To engage whole congregations in grasping the problems entailed in the contemporary distorted version of adolescence and wrestling with faithful responses.

- To resist assigning the task of youth ministry to a single person
  or small group except as these few become catalysts for engaging
  the entire congregation in faithful ways of relating with youth.

In these first two chapters, I have argued that adolescents in general and youth ministry in particular are limited by the expectations and pressures of culture. Indeed, seeing the problems clearly is easy enough. Fortunately, we are not left with empty cynicism, but a faith that calls forth hope. This faith shows us the importance of removing our naïve trust in culture and seeking more critical and creative ways of following God. In the chapter that follows I argue for reclaiming the Christian practice of discernment, as an appropriate model for youth ministry.

Notes

1. To domesticate something literally means to make it fit for the *domus* or home. When we domesticate animals and make them pets, we tame or limit their instincts that make them fit for the wild, and train them into patterns that are more convenient to our needs for companionship, cleanliness, safety, regularity, or entertainment. I am arguing that young people similarly have charisms that we have trained out of them, in our effort to make them fit our needs for security, regularity, or entertainment, or our greed. In particular, young people once held active social roles, but are now contained in more passive roles as students or consumers.

2. When Erik Erikson articulated the concept of adolescent moratorium, he had in mind a time of life in which young people experiment and explore the world, not one in which they are prevented from such exploration and experimentation. He observed the need for young people to more fully experience the messiness of life, not be removed from it. Erikson's concept of moratorium is often used today as a rationale for "warehousing" young people.

3. William Myers, *Black and White Styles of Youth Ministry: Two Congregations in America* (New York: Pilgrim Press, 1991), 57.

4. Ibid., 77.

5. America was among the nations that early rejected the feudal social arrangement of the aristocracy and peasantry in favor of a large middle class wielding modest power and influence instead of concentrating it in the hands of a few.

6. This and the above critique should not be seen as a rejection of education, but as a critique of the church that has not loudly enough or often enough insisted upon "love of God and neighbor" or a reconciling ethic that relieves education of its subservience to individualism and materialism, and places it in service of the reign of God and the common good. This is also not to suggest that young people of all classes should not be invited and challenged to use their intellects, or to pursue

professional success. But unless these pursuits are seen as ways for individuals to flourish and to sponsor the flourishing of others, through providing resources of justice to those in need, then as Jesus reminds us, those who find success may lose their souls.

7. Quentin J. Schultze, Roy M. Anker, James D. Bratt, William Romanowski, John W. Worst, and Lambert Zuidervaart, *Youth, Popular Culture, and the Electronic Media* (Grand Rapids: Eerdmans, 1991), 192.

8. PBS Video "The Merchants of Cool," original airdate: February 27, 2001. Produced by Barak Goodman and Rachel Dretzin, directed by Barak Goodman, written by Rachel Dretzin, correspondent and consulting producer Douglas Rushkoff. A FRONTLINE Co-Production with 10/20 Productions, LLC.

9. While the prevailing myth is apparently false that the average tenure of youth ministers is only eighteen months, most observers acknowledge that it remains relatively brief. In emphasizing the role of popular youth ministry in the turnover of youth ministers I do not want to ignore the diverse issues related to this brief tenure. In the research for *Youth Ministry That Transforms: A Comprehensive Analysis of the Hopes, Frustrations, and Effectiveness of Today's Youth Workers* by Merton P. Strommen, Karen Jones, and Dave Rahn (Grand Rapids: Zondervan, 2001), the authors uncovered several concerns troubling youth ministers, such as time conflicts between job demands and personal needs, time conflicts between administrative duties and the need for youth contact, a prevailing disconnect between students and the church to which they belong, a disinterested and apathetic youth group, a salary inadequate to support a family, and a youth budget too spare for needed programmatic activities. However, a close observer will recognize that these seemingly diverse problems have in common a confusion about the role of youth ministers — a role that isolates them from congregations, serves the dominant understanding about the priorities of youth and families, and sublimates the gospel and the vocation of youth beneath a host of cultural expectations.

10. Schultze et al., *Youth, Popular Culture*, 4.

11. Dorothy Bass and Don C. Richter, *Way to Live: Christian Practices for Teens* (Nashville: Upper Room Books, 2002).

Three

Reclaiming the Christian practice of discernment

Youth ministry seems poised in a *crisis* in which the cultural limits imposed on youth and ministers threaten to degrade human environments and further inhibit the fullness of God's reign. Also contained in this crisis, however, is an *opportunity* to relinquish our unreserved trust in contemporary culture and embody the beauty and wholeness we have glimpsed in a trustworthy God. If contemporary culture constrains youth, like an orange crate surrounding a young oak preventing its flourishing, then we might also admit it is unlikely that families or congregations can suddenly and decisively remove youth or themselves from this limiting culture and situate youth in a culture more conducive to their flourishing.

Few of us have the option of withdrawing like monastics from culture. Churches, families, and youth can never remove themselves entirely from the dynamics of culture, including the constantly shifting norms, values, and beliefs we generate in the course of negotiating our lives. This is true even for monasteries. Hard as we try, we never succeed once and for all in constructing a perfect culture, so that we can rest blissfully in its bosom. But if there is no way of stepping outside of culture, and no ideal culture for us to step into, then what are we to do? How do we create environments in which youth can grow in love of God and neighbor and into full selfhood? How do we help young people evaluate cultural expectations, cultivate their own gifts, and connect their stories to God's story? And how do we help youth ministers and congregations comprehend the problems and cultivate the potentials of adolescents?

In chapter 2, I used the analogy of a person attempting to grow an oak tree beneath an orange crate as a way of illuminating the constraints of contemporary culture and the possibilities of adolescent life. Another way to say much the same thing is that contemporary culture does not make a good "tree husband"; that is, culture remains largely inattentive to the flourishing of its young saplings. In consequence, the nurture of these young saplings should not be left to the husbandry of contemporary culture, but must become a shared responsibility among civil and religious institutions, and concerned citizens and religious individuals.

We can take this analogy a step further: growing a tree does not entail the once-for-all creation of some ideal environment in which saplings will automatically flourish. Trees do not spring fully and perfectly from the ground. Instead, growing a tree amounts to a years-long process, one that requires daily response to minute decisions. The gardener must think each day about when and how much to water, how to assure space for the roots, how to provide optimum sunlight, what types of soil and fertilizers are needed, how to prune, and how to extract insects and mosses that sap plant life. In other words, if we want to replace the limiting culture of the orange crate with a religious and cultural environment that encourages the tree to flourish, we need to do more than simply remove the crate. We also need to create something new, requiring for young people and their caregivers habitual decision-making skills or "skills of discernment." The art of making decisions is a crucial aspect of growing a tree and of cultivating Christian discipleship among young people.

Although Christians throughout history have faced oppression at the hands of various internal and external threats, contemporary commercial culture distorts human life in ways rarely encountered by the church. Yet we do not lack for resources from our Christian tradition. Congregations can reclaim the Christian practice of *discernment* to help contemporary youth cultivate skills for their growth in faith and to frame the activities of contemporary youth ministry. In particular, discernment in contemporary times must include refining our intuitions by the work of our minds, refining our thinking about the world by searching our souls in prayer, and enlarging our sense of compassion and wisdom by engaging in practical acts of faith in the world. This chapter illuminates some of the historical roots of the Christian practice of discernment. Subsequent chapters elaborate these four general movements of discernment — listening, understanding, remembering/dreaming, and acting — as an approach to youth ministry.

Contemporary culture's capacity for distorting life is unique in history, yet yearning to hear from God is not new. Neither, however, is self-deception, which hinders our hearing and following God. The practice of discernment assumes that God seeks to lead people to greater fullness and faithfulness. At the same time, discernment also recognizes that human sinfulness inhibits God's direction by confusing superficial distractions with our deepest desires to love God and neighbor. Although the means of discernment have varied through the centuries, God's people have long understood this struggle as central to a life of faith. The Bible and history are filled with stories of people seeking God's direction.

- In 1 Kings 3:9, Solomon pleads, "Give your servant therefore an understanding mind to govern your people, able to discern between good and evil."

- Romans 12:2 says, "Be transformed by the renewing of your minds, so that you may discern what is the will of God — what is good and acceptable and perfect."

- First Corinthians 12:10 says that God gives the gift of "discernment between spirits."

- First John 4:1 includes the injunction, "Do not believe every spirit, but test the spirits to see whether they are from God."

- Ephesians 1:18 includes the prayer of Paul: "I pray that the God of our Lord Jesus Christ may give you a spirit of wisdom and revelation as you come to know him, so that, with the eyes of your heart enlightened, you may know what is the hope to which he has called you."

From Moses' reception of the law on Mt. Sinai to Isaiah's hearing the small voice in the whirlwind, believers have always strained to hear how God would lead them to fullness and faithfulness. We might think, as well, of those Christian saints who similarly sought God's direction: Francis of Assisi, Teresa of Avila, St. Benedict, Mother Teresa, Archbishop Oscar Romero, Martin Luther, John Wesley, and Martin Luther King Jr. What distinguishes a saint seems to be no more nor less than his or her ability to discern and follow God's leading into places as unlikely as service to the poor, reform of the church and society, greater justice for the world, and a deeper love for God and neighbor.

Despite the exemplary path trod by these great saints and biblical legends, a sobering truth remains. No one person can ever discern God's leading or "hear" God with absolute perfection. From Abel's slighted ego prompting him to kill his brother Cain to King David's misappropriation of Uriah's wife, self-deception has distorted even our most faithful biblical heroes' ability to hear God's love and guidance clearly. So how then do we hear God? Through impressions in prayer? By reading and interpreting the Bible? Christian tradition? Human experience? Human reasoning? With the resources of the Christian community? And what are the sources of human distortion that inhibit our hearing and heeding? Are we hindered in hearing God by evil spirits? Fears? Ego structures? Seduction by sensual pleasure? Desire for approval? Or normalized social structures?

The history of discernment reflects the church's long struggle to understand how God reveals truth to humans amid our potential for distorting this truth. The various forms of discernment represent the diverse ways Christians have understood God's revelation of truth and the potential for human distortion. We can classify these different ways of discernment in four broad and overlapping categories that emphasize distinct human capacities — the work of the heart, mind, soul, and strength — as means of illuminating God's Word and resisting self-deceit: (1) discernment as a language of the heart that focuses on affect and intuition, through which God speaks;

(2) discernment as language of the mind, which engages in intellectual analysis, through which God speaks; (3) discernment as language of the soul, which privileges contemplation and biblical/theological imagination, through which God speaks; and (4) discernment as a language of the body, of practical exploration of the world, through which God also speaks. Let's look briefly at how Christians have historically sought God's direction for their lives.

Discernment as a language of the heart

Knowing God requires, first and foremost, that we listen to our heart. As Thomas Aquinas explained, if God is love, then the language of God cannot be fully rational. God speaks to the human heart in the language of emotion, so that our emotions constitute significant aids in our search for truth, allowing us to open ourselves more fully to God and neighbor. While contemporary culture and individual biases may colonize the rational mind, the heart can act as prophetic challenge, awakening humans to intuitions of evil and to God's irrational love. We know, for example, that while sound rational arguments are not insignificant, we are commonly moved to change by our emotions. We may recall, for example, that when numerous debates and closely reasoned legal judgments could not sway the entrenched racism of the South in the 1960s, a whole nation was finally moved to compassion witnessing scenes on television of black and white citizens being attacked when marching from Selma for civil rights. Discernment becomes possible whenever a person's sensitivity to one's "heart" makes one available to the Spirit's voice.

Where do we see heartfelt discernment in the early church? The New Testament contains numerous stories of Jesus's and the early Christians' confrontations with evil spirits, powers, and principalities, which the disciples were urged "to test." According to theologian Walter Wink, New Testament accounts of evil spirits can be interpreted as attempts to name the palpable evil or good intuited in the presence of relationships or institutions.[1] In essence, New Testament seers, mystics, and prophets accorded anthropomorphic (or demonic) qualities to *institutional* distortions — political, economic, and cultural "evils" of their own day. Wink argues that early Jewish and Christian worldviews understood earthly things as having an exact heavenly counterpart. He illustrates, "Each of the seven letters in chapters 2 and 3 of the book of Revelation are addressed, not to the congregation, as in the Apostle Paul's letters, but to the congregation's angel." He concludes, "The angel seemed to be the corporate personality of the church, its ethos or spirit or essence."[2] Within the first-century Roman occupation of Judea, for example, sensible or sensory intuitions of "legion" evil spirits were common experiences for many. He adds, "The 'powers that be' are not then simply people and their institutions, they also include the spirituality at the core of these institutions and structures."[3] Wink is not suggesting, however, that spirits are mere projections or illusions of internal human fears, but rather that spirits exist *as* the real spirituality of those systems and structures that have betrayed their divine vocations to foster human life.[4]

After the New Testament period, however, most worldviews tended to emphasize one reality and flatten the other.

- By the second century C.E., the spiritualistic worldview held that matter was evil and spirit was good. Having fallen from a good heaven, we are trapped in bodies and "subject to deformed and ignorant Powers that rule the world of matter."[5]

- The materialistic worldview was the antithesis of the spiritualist worldview and can be seen in writings as early as the fourth century B.C.E., but flourished in the Enlightenment of the seventeenth and eighteenth centuries. The materialistic worldview holds that all knowledge remains grounded in empirical and material certainties — what can be known by the five senses and reason — and by definition excluded the supernatural or spiritual realm.

- Finally, the modern theological worldview, as a compromise with Enlightenment rationalism, concedes material and earthly reality to modern science but preserves a spiritual realm immune to confirmation or refutation by the senses.

Wink argues for reclaiming an integrated worldview similar to that of the New Testament period, which understands every created thing or set of relationships as having both outer, visible structures and inner, spiritual realities. This integrated worldview corrects the dualisms of the spiritual, material, and theological worldviews, but is also in accord with a number of streams of thought — new physics, liberation theology, feminist theology, and the reflections of Carl Jung, Pierre Teilhard de Chardin, Alfred North Whitehead, Process Theology, Morton Kelsey, Matthew Fox, Native American religions, and Thich Nhat Hanh. We return to this integrated view later, but for now it is enough to grasp the importance of intuition or the language of the heart and its subsequent marginalization by post–New Testament thought.

Earlier, I noted that we generally appreciate art by taking in the *whole* work of music, painting, or dance as opposed to surveying the isolated elements of a given piece. Spiritual discernment as practiced by New Testament writers evinces a similarly attentiveness to *gestalts,* or to the overall feelings and impressions experienced in relationships with institutions, governments, economies, and societal structures. While early Christians surely used their intellects, they relied more heavily on heartfelt intuition than among the later Enlightenment that emphasized cognitive reason and analysis. We might summarize this sense of discernment in an expression: "You don't have to be an ichthyologist to smell a rotten fish!" Thus, although rational analysis provides important clues about the causes of deterioration, human sense, including intuition, provides information to warrant suspicion and avoidance. The Enlightenment represented an advance in the refinement of scientific methodology; unfortunately, however, it also occasioned a near-exclusive reliance on reason that obscured the value of intuition.

We also learn about the role of the heart in discernment from third- and fourth-century records of early Christian preparation for baptism. Candidates for baptism were taught Christian lifestyle practices by their communities before being taught a system of belief. Specifically, spiritual directors, through practices of discernment and exorcism, cleansed candidates of evil in preparation for baptism.[6] They may have used approaches similar to those employed by third-century theologian Origen, who taught people to use their intuition to discern the source of their thoughts. Origen recognized all human thoughts as having three sources: God, evil spirits, and good spirits. "If people could trace their thoughts, they could find a way to give themselves to the proper spirit, for people are always moved by the spirits to good or evil."[7] In the fourth century, John Cassian held similar views but added new criteria for testing thoughts to determine whether they moved a person toward good or evil: "(1) Is it filled with what is good for all? (2) Is it heavy with the fear of God? (3) Is it genuine in the feelings, which underlie it? (4) Is it lightweight because of human show or because of some thrust toward novelty? (5) Has the burden of vainglory lessened its merit or diminished its luster?"[8]

Subsequent centuries saw theologians refining the art of intuiting good and evil. By the sixteenth century, monks practicing discernment in accordance with rules drawn up by Ignatius Loyola daily asked themselves and one another, "Where is life and where is life draining from you?" in order to identify where God seemed to be at work. This Ignatian Examen focused attention in two ways: it prompted Christians to ask how God was accomplishing healing among them, bringing joy, life, exuberance, beauty, relationship, and glory; and it challenged them to explore how God seeks to heal the wounds of the world, particularly as these wounds are manifested in tension, antipathy, frustration, anger, suffering, death, and alienation. Making these judgments required a minimum of analysis but a maximum of intuition by the heart.

Despite its prevalence in early Christianity, intuition does not exhaust our options for practicing discernment. After all, few of us naturally possess impeccable intuition. Too often, our intuition can become a conduit for common sense, which in turn can hide cultural, and personal, biases. Instead intuition needs to be exercised like a muscle in order to maintain good decision making. Intuition thus requires cultivation by the mind, soul, and body in order to become a reliable conduit for wisdom. Additionally, while intuition may suffice for avoiding evil, transforming evil and restoring structures to their divine vocation for good requires a larger repertoire of skills. Walter Wink argues that, in order to identify and engage evil fully, we must recognize the real spiritual forces emanating from actual institutions. "Any attempt to transform a social system without addressing both its spirituality and its outer forms is doomed to failure. Only by confronting the spirituality of an institution and its concretions can the total entity be transformed."[9] While crucial for identifying distorted situations, intuition nevertheless requires additional support. To grasp the nature of cultural distortions and transform them, we must also analyze their concrete workings. Discerning the roots of evil requires, in short, that we use our minds and hearts together.

Discernment as a language of the mind

While the heart alerts us to palpable expressions of evil, the mind can analyze complex relationships, an ability that helps us identify causes and transform evil into good. If we want to be fully faithful, we must have accurate conceptual maps that chart the workings of the concrete world. It matters, for example, whether we view the created world as an endlessly exploitable resource or as a web of delicately balanced systems. It matters whether we see racism as the product of a few sick individuals or as encompassing deeply entrenched systems that deny some their full rights. And it matters whether we view urban poverty as the result of isolated cases of laziness or as the systematic withdrawal of resources from a community by banks and the corresponding white flight to the suburbs. In essence, making wise choices as partners with God in creating *shalom* requires skillful use of our intellects.

The necessity of employing intellectual powers to map the complexity of the world may seem obvious, but until the modern advent of the Enlightenment many perceived the workings of the world largely through intuitive means — through myth, superstition, or contemplation. The world seemed too mysterious and dangerous for the average person to discern accurately, and communities recognized a gifted few as possessing the capacity of discernment. From the fourth to the fifteenth centuries, for example, the Eastern church looked to the charisma of mystics and ascetics to illumine the truth of God. Seeking wisdom, people withdrew from the world and turned to desert fathers and mothers. For better and worse, the Enlightenment altered this frame of reference by introducing scientific methods for exploring the world and its complexity. The church often appeared deeply resistant to scientific method, which threatened its entrenched mythical perspectives. But increasingly, all the world's truth was viewed as God's, safe to explore with reasoning minds.

Reason thus became an important tool for understanding the world. But the translation of Enlightenment thought into religious or ecclesial arenas was not easily accomplished. Christians turned both inward to piety and outward to democracy as ways of retaining a fabric of religious meaning threatened by reason. Charismatic and pietistic traditions of discernment continued to enjoy popular appeal in Europe, even as some Enlightenment thinkers began viewing these traditions as unreliably dependent on the random in-breaking of the Spirit and on the authority of a sensitive minority. This kind of dependence conflicted with the democratic spirit of the Enlightenment. Thus while Eastern churches continued to rely on the charisma of a few, the Roman Catholic and later Protestant traditions began to deem individuals too deeply entangled in sin to serve as mystical conduits for God in their own right. Following the pattern of Roman law and styles of deliberation, the Western church instituted rational democratic processes for discerning truth. The English advent of the rule of law and Scottish parliamentary rules had enormous effects on discernment in European and American contexts. By the early nineteenth century, for example, many American churches adopted a faith that common people would discern truth if they possessed the relevant facts. Democratic government by the people, in other words, would hold in check the evil intentions of a few.[10] For much of the history of the Western church after the Enlightenment, group

decisions have relied on some variation of a process involving participants standing one at a time to present their argument and voting — a
form ultimately refined as parliamentary procedure or *Roberts Rules
of Order.* This style of deliberation allowed people to articulate diverse reasons and to persuade each other with arguments. Perhaps
more importantly, it also provided a systematic way for communities
to reach theological and practical conclusions.

Following centuries of violence among Western nation-states,
many European Christians hailed these orderly procedures in the
church and in the state as a breakthrough in mediating disputes. Yet,
however important these processes may have proved for minimizing
violence, the principle of majority rule effectively undervalued the
wisdom of the minority, through whom God often speaks. Although
community deliberations capably check the biases and distortions
of individuals, cultural biases can also distort corporate reasoning.
In cultures that validate the interests and perspectives of some and
ignore others, reason too finds itself distorted. God's truth may
in fact be an unpopular, minority opinion, scandalous to common
sensibilities.

In the twentieth century, Latin American base Christian communities raised questions from different perspectives than European or
American faith communities, which focused on personal and interpersonal sin. Base communities exercised a suspicion of social structures
and targeted economic, political, and social forces as distorters and
oppressors of human life. Discernment methods in these communities
vary, of course, but they invariably include empowering those among
the minority whose voices have been previously muted. The critical perspectives of these once-silenced people have challenged North
American Christians to examine complicated webs of power, money,
exploitation, and abuse that affect social organization. The discernment practice of Latin American base communities complements the
practice of intuition by comprehending powers and principalities or
by clearly identifying exploitation through reasoned analysis of social
and institutional patterns.

Discernment as a language of the soul

Reasoned analysis contributes important insights about the complexity of the societies in which we seek to be faithful. Despite its powers of analysis, however, reason can also become captive to the logic of distorted cultures. Reason, for example, figured large in creating the conditions for the Jewish holocaust, Stalinist genocide, and South African apartheid. These and other historical tragedies remind us that while intellect can investigate facts and give order to human experience, alone it cannot make meaningful judgments or generate values on its own terms. Divorced from intuition and compassion, reason cannot surface deep truths that emerge from the soul — such as the infinite worth of all humans and the presence of God among us.

To introduce the word "soul" is, of course, to suggest new possibilities for the practice of discernment. "Soul" can be defined in many different ways. Here I am using it to denote the deep resources of human experience where we touch the Holy. On this reading, "soul" indicates a call from beneath the unsettling distractions, tensions, and antipathies of life. Within the "still point" of the soul wisdom speaks to us in a manner qualitatively different from the immediate attractions of the heart or the exercises of the mind. Through prayer and contemplation, we connect to our deep experiences and memories of the Holy that lie beneath our expectations, whims, and fears.

In addition to being a source of our deepest values — love for God and neighbor — the soul also comprises the seat of the imagination. And imagination, in turn, realigns our perspectives in keeping with our deep knowledge of the Holy. Persons whose souls have been muted do not consider alternate possibilities beyond the status quo. But if prayer grounds us in the experience of love for God, theological reflection orients us in the story of God's dynamic work of love, and invites us to imagine ourselves part of that story in ways that transcend the status quo. This orientation is crucial in resisting cultural movements that distort created life and its goodness. For example, the myth of "the survival of the fittest" pervades science, business, and the military of our society, and if we are not to yield our imaginations to this myth, our reorientation in God's love and the story of God's love working through history is key. Soulful imagination challenges those cultural perspectives that reduce people to objects or competitors, and it reimages people as bearing the beauty of God and, as such, worthy of respect.

As two aspects of "soul," contemplation and imagination (remembering and dreaming) both concern themselves, in different ways, with reconciliation. They work to reunify and reconnect us in love to all creatures and to God. In the Christian tradition, contemplation and imagination correlate respectively to practices of prayer and to biblical/theological reflection, two activities central for proper discernment. Simply put, contemplation connects us to our deep experience of God through prayer, and imagination connects us to the story of God in which all are invited to participate.

Amid the confusions brought about by superficial distractions of the heart and mind, Christians can often turn to prayer as a source of humble clarity. Perhaps the most enduring form of prayer as Christian discernment remains the *Spiritual Exercises of Ignatius Loyola.* Ignatius devised "Rules for Discernment of Spirits" in which practitioners seeking discernment were asked to consider various rational alternatives to a given problem or dilemma. Practitioners were then instructed to allow these alternatives to "sound the depths of the soul" in prayer and contemplation, or to listen for echoes of truth in feelings of "consolation" or "desolation," which, Ignatius thought, either lead to God in peace or away from God in distress.

In the seventeenth and eighteenth centuries, Quakers made noteworthy contributions to prayer as a practice of discernment by engaging communities in prayerful listening for the "Inner Light," by which they meant the voice of the soul, specifically Christ within. As opposed to the Presbyterian or democratic procedures utilized by mainline churches, Quakers engaged groups not in debate and majority rule, but in prayer-laden discussions that built consensus. Even today in modern Quaker circles, such practices continue to assume that consulting the soul remains crucial as a context for reasoning, discussion, and debate. Quaker discernment allows for the possibility that truth sometimes appears most clearly in minority opinions — both the "small minority voice" speaking within the individual heart and those minority voices in the community.

Quaker discernment practices also permit a seeker to convene a "clearness committee" to help with decisions. The seeker may convene four or more people respected for their wisdom. These spiritual friends do not offer advice; they simply ask pertinent questions that prompt the seeker to think carefully about his or her dilemma and consider various practical, social, and spiritual factors. In raising important questions, the clearness committee invites the seeker's soul to wait for truth to emerge through prayer and silence. Quaker practice, like Ignatian discernment, advocates a strong role for the soul.

Especially in the Protestant tradition, the Bible has also stood as an important resource for those seeking to ground their lives in the depths of soul. If prayer cultivates our desire for reconciliation with God and creation, then so does God's story of love lure us from our isolation and bid us to join as partners in God's movement of reconciliation. If prayer provides roots to the soul, biblical and theological reflection gives wings to the imagination as we connect our lives to God's story of Love. The invention of the printing press by Johannes Gutenberg in 1450 c.e. introduced the Christian scriptures into the lives of many who had not enjoyed access to them previously. This allowed believers of varying traditions to claim scripture as a primary source of truth about God. In particular, the Protestant Reformation prompted an unprecedented common appeal to the authority of scripture. The protests sparked by Martin Luther, John Calvin, and Ulrich Zwingli emphasized that truth of scripture was accessible to the common person, and not reserved for priests alone. The Protestant movement gave momentum to a Counter-Reformation in the Catholic Church, which, partly out of its own internal sources of change and betterment, formalized Catholic dogma to accommodate the popular yearning for spiritual guidance and interest in scripture as well as tradition and authority. Although neither Catholic nor Protestant Christians agree completely about how to interpret and apply holy scripture, both groups of believers persist in comprehending their lives through the stories, metaphors, and injunctions contained in the Bible, particularly those that illuminate the life and work of Jesus.

The Bible has thus figured prominently in practices of discernment. Not only has it been used on occasion as a source of literal injunctions, but its rich images and metaphors also open us to alternate ways of imagining the world and our place in it. Ignatius Loyola's practice of discernment, for example, included the exercise of our imagination in relation to the story of God's grace in Jesus. These scriptural meditations move from Christ's birth and childhood, through his public ministry, to his passion, death, and resurrection. The Ignatian seeker spends much time allowing images of Jesus's life and death to suffuse his imagination. Their imaginations so suffused, they are provoked to identify with Jesus and participate in his passion and the redemption of the world — as they perceive their own opportunities for crucifixion and resurrection, and their judgments gradually conform to the story and logic of Jesus.

Christian faith as expressed and cultivated in the "soul practices" of prayer and biblical/theological reflection provide an important center from which Christians can evaluate their many choices in life. But when we ignore the dynamic relationship between these sources, we find ourselves living with new distortions. Prayer without recognition of biblical/theological resources risks isolating us from a story-formed community identified with God's work in history. Conversely, biblical and theological imagination apart from prayer and contemplation can lead to vain imagining — for example, Karl Barth characterized theologians as "bats and owls squabbling about the noonday sun."[11] But when held together in dialectic tension, these soul resources strengthen each other and provide clues to God's guidance.

Discernment as a language of action

At least since the medieval period, the church has recognized that how we live has relevance for what we know. Thomas á Kempis, author of the fifteenth-century classic *The Imitation of Christ,* assumed that living faithfully after Christ's example would generate godly wisdom. Thomas recognized that truth cannot be known in abstraction from our action in the world; instead, truth announces itself to us as we pursue a particular way of life. Quite simply, if we imitate Christ, then truth becomes self-evident in a manner that cognitive or emotional discernment alone cannot achieve. Hence, how we act in the world has enormous relevance for our hope to discern truth.

In recent years, increasing recognition of how commercial culture distorts our lives has prompted some writers to call for renewed attention to the imitation of Jesus.[12] Such a task is easier said than done, of course. Although we want to shape our lives so that they adhere to our faith, too often our lives remain habitually structured by cultural activities that distract us from imitating Jesus's practices. Most contemporary Christians, after all, still have to drive, shop, consume goods, and so forth. Many of us also choose to watch television and go to movies. Our cultural activities — both those that remain unavoidable and those that we select as entertainment — require and promote character traits that sometimes compete with our commitments to be like Jesus. Habits of contemporary life often evoke narcissism, individualism, competition, and viewing each other as objects. In our fast-food culture, for example, eating functions to refuel our on-the-go bodies, but for Jesus, taking food was an opportunity to gratefully acknowledge the Creator, the bounty of the earth, those who grew and prepared the food, and to share bounty with friends and strangers. Fast-food culture isolates and alienates. While we may view cashiers and cooks as invisible functionaries, Jesus's practice with food and table brought respect, gratitude, praise, community, responsibility, and care.

If we organize our lives around Jesus's practices of showing hospitality to strangers, taking and blessing food, respecting others, truth-telling, Sabbath keeping, and care of the earth, the values embodied in these practices emerge as wisdom to direct our life choices. When we engage these practices, we internalize ideas, sensibilities, and commitments that direct our future choices. Individual Christian journeys potentially evolve into greater fullness as we follow God's leadings, and as we embody God's Way these leadings become increasingly clear. As we live in the way we know to be faithful, God leads us into greater faith. Failure to live according to our knowledge of faithfulness hinders the potential for new and greater faithfulness.

Acting faithfully is important for another reason. We certainly grasp wisdom through the receptive faculties of our hearts, minds, and souls, but we also — perhaps even more so — learn wisdom from our practical movements in the world of concrete things and people. Just as athletes learn proficiency by training their bodies to work with their minds and hearts, so does fullness of faith require the disciplined habit of deliberate integration of our capacities. As we deploy our faith in the world, we learn to follow our hearts, trust our minds and souls, and extend our bodies in God's project of love. Smooth integration of all these faculties does not come easily or in abstraction; it comes through acting faithfully. We may have the best of intentions and impeccable theology, but these do not guarantee that our attempts at faithfulness will flourish. Only reflective practice in the complex world of concrete bodies, practical exigencies and interrelationships over time can cultivate the faithfulness that we seek. Negotiating faith within these realities produces practical wisdom that can be brought to bear in discernment.

Conclusions

From age to age people of faith have sought to know and respond to God based on their understandings of God, self, and others. But as Walter Wink reminds us, these understandings rely to a large degree upon the worldviews of given periods. While New Testament society held an integrated worldview emphasizing continuity between the concrete world and spiritual realities, only later would Enlightenment thinkers systematize the science of analysis for grasping the complexities of social, political, and physical realities. Premodern worldviews upheld a vision of disembodied spirits that governed human life, leaving discernment for mystical and prophetic intuition rather than reason. Some progressive Christians responded to Enlightenment by valorizing reason and relegating intuition, theological imagination, and practical wisdom to the margins of religious life. Fundamentalist Christians deal with the encroachment of modern rationalism by attempting to retreat into premodern spirituality that resists scientific interpretations of the concrete world. Finally, in whatever age, negotiating the assumptions of culture is a tricky business, yet the Christian church cannot simply ignore culture or its assumptive worldviews. As we have seen, sometimes these worldviews help the church while other times they distort our view of life and our place in it. At best, we see through a dark glass and any claims of absolute certainty should be suspect. Discerning God's way forward should always be, among other things, a matter of humility.

While no broad typological presentation of history can capture the complexity of events and ideas as they actually evolved, it remains crucial to try to keep in mind some sense of our place in history. Understanding the past is particularly necessary if we want to consider future practices of discernment. How does our historical context influence how we practice discernment today? What does it mean to discern truth in postmodernity as compared to modernity or premodernity? What are the risks and benefits of being church and doing youth ministry in a postmodern era?

The recognition of the cultural sea change called postmodernism has sparked much debate, in part because some see postmodernism as a significant problem to be solved while others find it a self-evident good that overturns the tyranny of abstract reason and other biases. While I have not entered the postmodern debate directly, throughout our discussion thus far I have highlighted what I view as the dangers and risks of postmodern commercial culture for youth and their congregations. Postmodern commercial culture generally shapes youth as consumers, alienating them from their hearts, minds, souls, and bodies. Postmodern commercial and political cultures have alienated young people from the wisdom of their communities and from their intrinsic gifts for God's reign. But although some aspects of postmodern culture have certainly given rise to alienation, others in postmodern philosophy have rightly made us aware of our need for relationships and connections.

While we cannot diminish the trials and hardships of early Christians, the issues facing the postmodern world are vastly more complex than those concerns facing early Christian disciples. Unlike those of early Christians, the influences that demand our attention are not limited to a handful of interpersonal relations or as obvious as threats by imperial or tyrannical rulers, but today include webs of interconnecting economic, political, and environmental relationships over the globe. Today, we are increasingly aware, for example, that our actions do matter to the rest of the world, and that what happens across the continent or globe does affect us. Events in Hollywood, Wall Street, Israel, the Amazon rainforest, Afghanistan, and even Antarctica affect our lives directly. Within the small, relatively self-sufficient communities prevalent throughout preindustrial history, persons did not ask such questions of globalization and its effects. Today, however, we cannot avoid such questions when seeking to participate in God's salvation. When we become aware of how global interrelationships are essential to our wholeness, and how our postmodern commercial habits alienate us from each other, creation, and our true selves, we are essentially thinking in new ways about the nature of truth and discernment.

As observed by countless scholars, in modernity, truth became identified with isolated, objective, or dead "facts," an association that treated the world as an object to be dissected and manipulated. Modern thinkers abstracted factual truth from creation's yearning for wholeness, from its heart, soul, and body. In modernity, in short, "truth" amounted to whatever an individual could use in a functional way to advance his or her interests and perspectives. In the hands of engineers, industrialists, and politicians, this kind of knowledge produced the isolation, loneliness, violence, fear, and threats of the nuclear age. Knowledge as sheer curiosity and control distanced us from one another and creation and has carried us to the brink of nuclear death.

In the divergence of postmodern theory from modern technical rational methods of knowledge, it offered new insights into the nature of truth. Parker Palmer, for example, advocates reclaiming a form of truth that originates not in an intellectual heritage that privileges curiosity or control, but in our spiritual heritage, a place in which knowledge arises from love to reunify and reconstruct broken selves and worlds. "In Christian tradition, truth is not a concept that works but an incarnation that lives," Palmer argues. "The 'Word' our knowledge seeks is not a verbal construct but a reality in history and the flesh.... Not an objectified system of empirical objects in logical connection with each other, but an organic body of personal relations and responses, a living and evolving community of creativity and compassion."[13] As a personal God knows and loves us in a personal way, so do we come to know and love in this same manner. Palmer reminds us that the Germanic root for the word "truth" also gives rise to our word "troth" as in the ancient wedding vow, "I pledge thee my troth."

> To know something or someone in truth is to enter troth with the known, to rejoin with new knowing what our minds have put asunder. To know in truth is to become betrothed, to engage the known with one's whole self, an engagement one enters with attentiveness, care and good will. To know in truth is to allow one's self to be known as well, to be vulnerable to the challenges and changes any true relationship brings. To know in truth is to enter into the life of that which we know and to allow it to enter into ours. Truthful knowing weds the knower and the known; even in separation, the two become part of each other's life and fate.[14]

Parker further explains that knowledge "springs from a love that will implicate us in the web of life, wrap the knower and known in compassion, and a bond of awesome responsibility and transforming joy, and call us to involvement, mutuality and accountability."[15] Put differently, while my senses discriminate and my mind dissects, my prayer acknowledges and recreates the unity of life. In prayer, I no longer set myself apart from others and the world, manipulating them to suit my needs. Instead, I reach for relationship, allow myself to feel the tugging of mutuality and accountability, take my place in community by knowing the transcendent center that connects it all.[16]

Palmer calls us to discern truth in a manner that invites the mind into relationship with the heart, soul, and body. In his view, discernment is not an isolated or abstracted endeavor, but requires relationship with diverse others across the globe, with our broken creation, and with our communities in which we seek wholeness. And as always, it simultaneously requires integration within the individual, or between one's heart, mind, soul, and body.

Palmer's understandings mirror feminist postmodern theories that call for a deeper integration or connection-making between our minds, hearts, souls, bodies, and the world. Palmer's understandings also recall Wink's recognition of an integrated worldview that sees the holy mysteries of life embedded deeply in life's systems and structures, not confined to a distant realm, whether heavenly, spiritual, material, or theological. Wink, like Palmer, recognizes discernment as a more complex proposition in postmodernity than recognized by other worldviews in which truth could be sensed in one place or the other, through one faculty or the other. Discernment in these postmodern times must include refining our intuitions by the work of our minds, refining our thinking about the world by searching our souls with prayer, and enlarging our sense of compassion and wisdom by engaging in practical acts of faith with wounded others in the world. Those who deliberately practice these forms of discernment cultivate a deep sense of truth and refine their intuitions about truth. Truth becomes deeply ingrained in our bones, not remaining an abstract idea. It instead develops into a dynamic relationship between our hearts, minds, souls, bodies, and the world around us as we move ever beyond ourselves toward greater relatedness and truth.

Athletes practice fundamental skills — dribbling, shooting, swinging, winding up, teeing off — to make these skills "second nature," to integrate their hearts, minds, souls, and bodies toward a single purpose. So must we be deliberate in our practice of relational truth that can renew and transform us from faith to greater faith. In the view of Enlightenment rationalism, we prepare for faithful action by refining our thoughts about God and the world. In this integrated postmodern view, the manner in which we seek truth stands as continuous with the relational nature of truth itself. We do not prepare to become faithful by simply thinking well about faith, but by practicing faithfulness in fullness — heart, mind, soul, and body. If the reign of God includes harmony among all nations, tribes, and tongues, surely it also includes integration of individuals in true and full selfhood.

Theologian Søren Kierkegaard insists with Jesus that duplicity can never be a faithful act: "We cannot love God and mammon." Purity of heart means willing one thing: love of God and neighbor.[17] This integrated approach to discernment requires that the distractions of the heart, the whims of the body, and the hubris of the mind be refined by the intuitions of the heart, investigations of the mind, the still point of the soul, and the practical wisdom of the body. Just as a skillful athlete or a winning team continually refines unnecessary habits until all actions form a unified purpose, so are we called to refine our lives in the way of Jesus. We may never have a complete view of truth, but as our relationships become more secure in the way of love we will see partial truth emerging before us.

As we discovered in earlier chapters, adolescence in the twenty-first century is a particularly distorted situation. Young people stand increasingly isolated from their own intuitions, their intellectual curiosity about the world, their souls that seek to love God and heal the broken world, and from their own agency, resources required to resist domestication amid a hostile culture. This fragmentation only intensifies when we recognize young people's isolation within their communities. The kind of healing that the gospel calls for requires not simply a change of ideology, nor an emotional experience, though these may be important. *The healing needed among youth demands that we introduce them to practices of discernment that engage their whole selves.*

In the deliberate practice of discernment, young people will seek to be faithful in the hundreds of minute decisions that face them. As a young oak is nurtured, one decision at a time, into fullness, so discernment creates an incrementally adequate environment for growth in Christian vocation, or love of God and neighbor. One decision at a time, the orange crate of culture that limits our young people's growth can be dismantled and discarded, and youth will finally find more appropriate — and genuine — ways to support their flourishing as disciples and saints.

Notes

1. Walter Wink, *Engaging the Powers: Discernment and Resistance in a World of Domination* (Minneapolis: Fortress Press, 1992), 4ff.

2. Walter Wink, *The Powers That Be: Theology for a New Millennium* (New York: Doubleday, 1999), 3.

3. Ibid, 4.

4. Wink, *The Engaging the Powers,* 4–9.

5. Wink, *The Powers That Be,* 16.

6. Danny Morris and Charles Olsen, *Discerning God's Will Together: A Spiritual Practice for the Church* (Nashville: Upper Room, 1997), 49–76.

7. Ibid., 26.

8. Ibid., 27.

9. Wink, *Powers That Be,* 10.

10. Morris and Olsen, *Discerning God's Will Together,* 34.

11. Karl Barth, *Anselm: Fides Quaerens Intellectum,* trans. Ian W. Robinson (London: SCM, 1960), 27.

12. See, for example, Dorothy C. Bass, *Practicing Our Faith: A Way of Life for a Searching People* (San Francisco: Jossey-Bass, 1998).

13. Parker Palmer, *To Know as We Are Known: Education as a Spiritual Journey* (San Francisco: HarperSanFrancisco, 1993), 14.

14. Ibid., 31.

15. Ibid., 9.

16. Ibid., 11.

17. Søren Kierkegaard, *Purity of Heart* (New York: Harper Perennial, 1956).

Part two

Practicing discernment in your setting

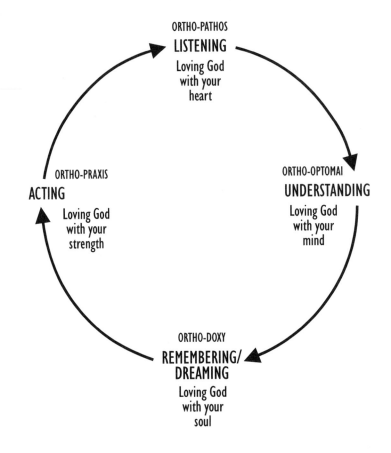

ORTHO-PATHOS
LISTENING
Loving God
with your
heart

ORTHO-OPTOMAI
UNDERSTANDING
Loving God
with your
mind

ORTHO-DOXY
**REMEMBERING/
DREAMING**
Loving God
with your
soul

ORTHO-PRAXIS
ACTING
Loving God
with your
strength

Discernment, as it has been practiced by Christians, involves seeking ways to know God's will and to join in partnership with God. Christians have explored various ways of knowing God's will — ranging from attention to their hearts, or minds, or souls, or bodies. Different Christian communities have emphasized these differently and few have integrated them all in systematic ways. This approach to youth ministry seeks to integrate them in an organic fashion, connecting them to each other. This illustration shows the four movements of discernment that can be practiced with youth in your setting. Practice of discernment in the way elaborated here joins youth in partnership with God and engages them in healing the world.

Four

Listening

Loving God with your heart —
Movement one

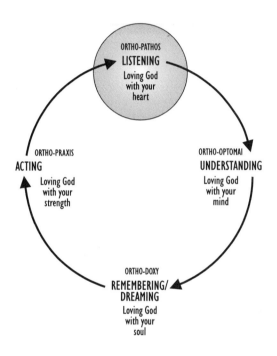

"Katie, I've told you a dozen times, I don't have money for all the frivolous things you want! And besides you have lots of jeans already!" explained Jackie Simpson, the exasperated mother of a disappointed teen.

"But, Mom, these jeans are not frivolous. All the girls are wearing them. I look like so nineties in my old jeans.... They come all the way up to my waist," argued Katie. "You don't want me to be an outcast, do you? You wouldn't buy me a car when I turned sixteen, like all my friends' parents. You wouldn't buy me that bracelet the other day...and you hardly ever let me go with my friends to the movies. My friends are going to abandon me!"

"Kate, I understand your desire to be like your friends and to be liked by your friends, but do we have to buy that approval?" pleaded her mother. "Aside from not having the money to fund your MTV lifestyle, I'm afraid that you are letting your friends determine who you are — what you look like, what you do, what you want and think. When will you learn to think for yourself?" Katie hung her head and tried to let her mother's words sink into her heart, but as much as she tried she could only feel the intense pressure of her friends' judgment upon her.

Shifting from reasoned authority to compassion, more appropriate to her true feelings for her daughter, Jackie asked tearfully, "I just want to know where that little girl is — the one that I raised, who used to love life, run in the park, explore the flowers, climb trees, swim in the lake, dance ballet and devour every Bible story I read to her? You seem to have lost your passion for ordinary life. Where did it go, Katie?"

"I'm not a little girl anymore, Mom. I just want to fit in with my friends...and they just wouldn't understand swimming in the lake or reading the Bible," she replied, her tears now speaking as loudly as her words.

"What do you really want from life, Katie...I mean, in addition to pleasing your friends?" asked her mom.

"I don't know, Mom," Katie sighed.

This struggle between Katie and her mother represents a common tension in American homes, in which youth culture recruits young people and draws them away from their families and the deepest yearnings of their hearts. The incessant distractions of fashion and entertainment commodities manipulate the desires of teens, seducing them to habits of consumption, distracting them from their hearts' call to love and compassion. While the distractions of commodity consumption are not the only or worst sins that seduce young people, they play a particular role among youth by obscuring desires — making holy desires difficult to remember, and distorted desires difficult to acknowledge and resist. Christian faith requires disciples of Jesus to cultivate skills for listening to our hearts as a means of resisting forces that, whatever their source, distract us from desires appropriate to our humanity from love of God and neighbor.

As emphasized in the exchange between Katie and her mother, youth culture plays a key role in distracting young people from their hearts. The practice of listening to one's heart helps young people to pay attention to situations that give them life and promote love. Recalling these activities and situations can be important in helping youth to seek vocation as agents of God, especially in a culture that is hostile to Christian faith.

This seduction of teens by commodity culture gains advantage in part because we have grown to expect it and imagine that it has always been the case. While many have viewed commodity attraction as a natural, quaint, and harmless part of growing up, historian Grace Palladino argues that the pattern of consumption in youth has historical roots — and that parents and teachers have not always thought it so harmless.[1] Prior to the 1930s, many youth in the largely agricultural communities of early twentieth-century America held significant social roles where they worked alongside adults and moved easily into adulthood without the prolonged state of beleaguered limbo that youth of today endure. With the Great Depression of the 1930s, youth found themselves pushed out of work on family farms and relegated to high schools, which became the new defining institution of adolescence. While in 1929 only 20 percent of all youth attended American high schools, by the end of the 1930s the percentage had risen to almost 80 percent. Marketers soon realized that youth confined to high schools were ready targets for commercial exploitation and began to advertise fashionable commodities such as sweaters, jackets, and school rings in scholastic journals. Although parents and teachers initially protested the commercial exploitation of their youth, they eventually capitulated to these marketers. After

all, the marketers argued, they weren't simply hawking cool jackets and rings, but a means of softening the impact of newly enforced
high school attendance standards. Teachers and parents came to view
fashion and entertainment commodities as a means for keeping youth
in school long enough to secure credentials for middle-class employment. In one brief generation, families experienced a shift from
youth generating income to draining income from their parents. Significantly, the newly autonomous youth culture became organized
around values of consumption, image, and conformity — often at
odds with traditional values of their local communities.

Today, the business of targeting youth as consumers has grown to
enormous proportions. Consumer pressures virtually define the institution of adolescence, with detrimental consequences for young
people. This virtual world of consumer culture presents to youth
a chimera of happiness that temporarily numbs their ache for God
and neighbor. Commodity promotion and consumption intrude with
such ubiquity and force that it is nearly impossible for youth to hear
the whispers of their own hearts. Commodity producers manipulate
the desires of young people, exploiting them for profit. Marketers
constantly urge young people to view their products, ranging from
toothpaste to clothing, as essential for gender identity, belonging, or
happiness, creating artificial mini-crises that prompt an endless cycle
of self-dissatisfaction and consumption to relieve this engineered dis-
satisfaction. Today, the average teen, through television, billboards,
Internet pop-up ads, magazines, and other media, views over three
thousand advertisements each day. But if desires are colonized by advertising, so is personal space colonized by the flurry of electronic
gadgets that diminish the silence or solitude in which young people
might listen to their hearts. Consequently, the adolescent heart that
feels compassion on behalf of those suffering and loves the ordinary
goodness of life — relationships, curiosity, creativity, work, play, community, and the Holy — often becomes suppressed into near silence.
Today, many youth have become so enamored of their consumer
lifestyles that vocation as defined by Frederick Buechner — "where

deep gladness meets the world's deep hunger"[2] — now stands as severely inhibited, because the average teenager knows little of deep gladness or the world's hunger. While the institution of adolescence has engaged teens in distraction, conformity, and consumption, obscuring their love for God and neighbor, the stories of individual youth and exceptional groups are not so dire. Fortunately, the social forces inhibiting adolescent faith are never totalizing without remainder, because there always remains alive some part of us that yearns for love. In fact, as any parent, teacher, or youth minister knows, curiosity, faith, creativity, camaraderie, and compassion remain strong in youth. And yet, there is much that could be done to support these gifts of youth and help more youth to resist forces that inhibit them. The potential of youth to live authentic Christian life in its fullness depends upon deliberate practices of resisting forces that mute their love for God and neighbor, and supporting those that enhance love.

The aim of discernment is as Aristotle advocated, to have the right feelings at the right time — or ortho-pathos.

Listening to the heart in Christian theology

While Christian theology has always held in its deepest veins the centrality of the heart, the church has sometimes viewed passions and emotions with suspicion, as sources of unworthy or dangerous drives. In part, this is because passion threatens the predictability of the rational life. Also the Christian church too often has assumed that right doctrines or ideas alone guard faithfulness. Our cognitive bias has allowed us to ignore the role of the heart in Christian faith, yet the Bible views the heart as a source of both distortion and healing, with potential for opening or closing us to love.

The Bible's frequent use of the metaphor "heart" reveals a coiled spring that gives rise to emotions, passions, drives, or energies as fundamental sources of ethical and spiritual life.[3] The heart plays a profound role in the Christian story, grounded in God's suffering or the passion of Christ. In the Gospel accounts, Jesus reveals a passionate God compelled by love, living life richly from his heart, as he smiled upon children, wept with Martha and Mary, flashed anger at the money-changers, and demonstrated compassion for lepers. These accounts reveal Jesus's heart open to love of God and neighbor — giving and vulnerable, not hardened by fear or idolatry. A deep and abiding love motivated Jesus's costly gift of himself and became the raison d'être of the church. By entering into the passionate and self-giving love that animated Jesus, we also enter more fully into true selfhood, the purpose for which we were created. This passion embraces both the delights and pains of love — delight as we celebrate relatedness and blessing, pain when human flourishing is prevented by acts of injustice or self-deception.

But the biblical testimony also reveals the potential for hearts to become distracted or separated from love of God and neighbor. In Exodus, we are told that Egypt was punished for the hardness of Pharaoh's heart against the Israelites and God (Exod. 7:13, 14, 22; 8:15, 19, 32; 9:7, 12, 34, 35). In the Gospel of Mark, Jesus warns the Pharisees and his own disciples to take care lest they harden their hearts to God (Mark 6:52; 8:17). Matthew's Gospel warns us of the potential for our hearts to attach to inordinate desires; that is, wherever our treasures are stored, whether in mammon or God, there will our heart be (Matt. 6:21). Matthew makes it clear that "what we love" remains central to the quality of our relationships with God and neighbor. We stand responsible for the objects of our desire, those things to which our hearts become attached. Some desires open us more fully to God and to neighbor, while others distract us from these greater goods, perverting our love of God, neighbor, and our true self.

The Bible reveals a remedy for hardness of the heart in feeling our grief. In *The Prophetic Imagination*, Walter Brueggemann finds in the Pentateuch an appeal to the heart for reclaiming right relationships.[4] He insists that prophetic ministry begins not with "carping and denouncing" the powers of dominant culture, but instead with grieving. Only by first *feeling* our grieving hearts can we make the most visceral announcement that things are not right. In the story of the exodus from Egypt, Israel gave public expression to its hurt as an important first step in dismantling the powers that be, thus making room for a new reality to emerge.

> And the people of Israel groaned under their bondage, and cried out for help, and their cry under bondage came up to God. And God heard their groaning, and God remembered his covenant.... And God saw the people of Israel, and God knew their condition. (Exod. 2:23–25)

Brueggemann argues that such a primal cry from the heart reoccurs as an animating dynamic throughout the Bible, as time and again people with whom God has made covenant yearn for freedom.

Theologians have argued that the heart is not only significant for its potential to distort, but through suffering and delight draws us to fullness of life and faith. Thomas Aquinas reminds us that God is Love and the best way to know God is not through the mind, but through the heart.[5] We cannot fully comprehend God through intellectual investigation or logical analysis, but through the heart we can have reliable knowledge of God. According to Thomas, God has created all creatures out of the very fabric of God's own self and shares love and being with all in the form of their simple existing, in the uniqueness of their existence. Thus to fulfill our nature — to satisfy the very purpose of our being — is to engage in loving and being loved as we are caught up in the love of God. Each day, we experience numerous occasions for compassion capable of drawing us out of ourselves, softening our hardened hearts, and drawing us into love with others and God. Too often we repress these epiphanies or invitations in favor of familiar and safe patterns, but we do so at the risk of losing the capacity for love of God and the world. Such a view of the dynamics of faith requires us to move beyond a mere emphasis on orthodoxy as right knowing, to embrace an ortho-pathos as right feeling — including practices of listening to our hearts and teaching youth to do the same.

The practice of listening

Having grasped the importance of helping young people to resist cultural and personal distortions by listening, and having briefly elaborated the theological significance of listening, what does this practice look like? What specifically are the aims of a practice of listening? And how might this practice be appropriated for ministry with youth? As mentioned earlier, an aim of listening is to cultivate feelings appropriate to our situations — ortho-pathos. Listening to our hearts creates the possibility of studying our hidden and unhidden motives and responses, and the world in which they occur, for the purpose of creating more space for love to be expressed in the world, and less space for fearful or obsessive reactions that limit life and love. A practice of listening might have allowed Katie to study her fear of being alienated from friends, her attraction to fashion, her repulsion at her mother's hopes, and her own secret pleasures of swimming and Bible stories — to better understand how these fears and pleasures were distorted. Acknowledging feelings and the situations in which they occur represents opportunity for critical and theological reflection and active participation with God's work in the world. For example, feelings of love or vitality may point to important relationships or signature gifts that should be fostered. Anger may, for example, point to social structures that support racism or gender injustice. Sadness may point to educational systems and the limitations they represent for young people who yearn to engage their gifts in the healing of the world. Listening for these emotions in the hearts of youth may provide motivation for agency of faith in the world's transformation.

The practice of listening allows space for young people's hearts to speak, to make known their fears or hopes or loves. Any practice that facilitates expression of emotion is potentially important for youth ministry. Yet, there are some occasions in which feelings are clear and unequivocal, and others in which they are not fully available to consciousness, their heart's so guarded and covered over by defenses that more subtle practices are required to surface feelings.

Most teenagers can name situations in which they feel anger or sadness about, for example, being rejected by friends or being benched by the basketball coach. However, many youth are only dimly aware of deeper fears of not being accepted by others or not finding within one's life any gift of worth. Some tensions emerge as only a vague awareness or knot in the stomach. Surfacing deeply protected feelings may require attention to the unconscious or preconscious and can be accomplished through art, drama, dreamwork, guided meditation, or other approaches for probing these depths.

When we attend to our hearts, we can learn much about our location in the world. When we attend to our feelings, we may find ourselves better able to understand our formation in family contexts, the structures of our society, injustices in the world, and significantly, the possibilities for God's transformation of these contexts. A stiff neck, for example, may constitute a significant comment about one's financial situation, work context, family dysfunction, or the fear of war in the Middle East. The practice of paying attention to these tensions stands as a way of gaining understanding about our world, the ways we have been shaped by our world, and the possibility of shaping our lives and our world in more beautiful ways responsive to God's reign. Attending to these tensions helps us to claim responsibility in the world as agents responsive to God and our neighbors.

Yet, tensions and distortions do not represent the full range of our hearts' experience. It is equally crucial to observe places of joy, peace, fullness, connection, glory, and creativity — or as Ignatius Loyola named them, the "consoling passions." If the Spirit's work involves reconciling all things, then we need to pay attention whenever beauty and flourishing appear on our horizons, in order that we might support these gifts and be grateful. The practices of "counting your blessings" and "giving testimony" constitute ways in which Christians historically have acknowledged God's work among them. Moreover, as we attend to our experiences of peace, joy, beauty, and wholeness, we may find in these reflective moments important clues to Christian vocation — how God may be calling us as partners in the world's healing.

Identifying generative heart themes

In addition to making us self-aware, an aim of listening is to help problematize situations, to lift them from their context and analyze their meaning, to make them a problem to be solved. Problematizing begins by identifying particular situations in the various contexts of adolescent life — school, home, work, peer groups, church — in which young people are "pushing past apathy," where they are sad, angry, frustrated, joyful, ecstatic, or content. These emotions emerge within a range of human situations that represent opportunities to participate with God in transforming or supporting these situations.

When building an approach to youth ministry around the movement of Listening, it is important for a youth group to create a list of heart themes that are common to the group. Heart themes are simply ways for groups to capture the reality of particular situations in which there is much emotion. A heart theme involves some *expression of emotion* and some brief *description of a context*. The following represent examples of heart themes that surface among youth.

Expression of emotion	*Description of context*
Youth feel *frustrated about*	*exclusion from church leadership roles.*
Youth *appreciate*	*working alongside older adults in mission projects.*
Youth feel *tense about*	*competition they experience in relation to fellow students.*
Youth feel *sad because*	*parents do not spend time with them.*
Youth *enjoy*	*participating as liturgical leaders in congregational worship.*

These themes should not be seen as universal, but as describing the feelings of particular young people in particular contexts. Behind each of these generative themes there are rich stories of young people and their world.

Practical approaches to listening for themes

Here are some ways various youth groups have worked to surface heart themes.

Small groups

One way to identify the heart themes or emotional energies of youth is to host a church event with the focused goal of listening to youth. Some congregations host a series of potlucks or a day-long Saturday workshop to discuss the issues peculiar to youth, including young people's relationship with church and community. Still others host clusters of home meetings in various church neighborhoods. Congregations or youth groups can implement the following steps to promote the telling of and listening to the stories of youth.

1. Ask the youth to form groups of three.

2. Ask each group of three to discuss and record on newsprint their answers to one of the following questions. Each group of three should be assigned a different question.

   a. "What are your hopes and your worries about the church and this community?"

   b. "What are the main problems or tensions you experience in this church and this community?"

   c. "What are the main problems or tensions you experience in school?"

   d. "What are the main problems or tensions you experience at work?"

   e. "What are the main problems or tensions you experience with friends?"

   f. "Where do you experience joy?" and "Where do you feel most alive?"

3. Allow ten to fifteen minutes for discussion in small groups.

4. Ask each group to highlight the three most urgent hopes, problems, tensions, or worries of their group.

5. When each small group finishes, ask them to return to the large group. Allow each group to verbally share the items they highlighted on their list and to fill in any additional descriptions of their themes.

6. As a large group, look for common themes among the lists presented.

7. Ask the large group of youth to identify the most important issues for future discussion.

Timed writing

Sometimes when simple discussion fails to elicit feelings or when people seem too guarded, timed writing exercises can help bring feelings to the surface. In a timed writing exercise, young people are given paper, a writing instrument, a topic, and a time limit of from three to five minutes. They are instructed to put their pens to the surface of the paper and not to stop writing until the time has elapsed. They are told that if they cannot think of any relevant insight they should simply keep writing, for example, "I cannot think of anything to write," until a thought returns. The topics for their writing can be framed in a number of ways to elicit their feelings. For example, a common topic is, "What makes me the most angry about my home life is..." Other topics that may elicit emotion for young people include peer or romantic relationships, demands of school, pressures of parents, and expectations of future work. Once timed writings have been completed, ask participants to simply name the themes that emerge in their writing or to draw a picture to illustrate their themes or possibly to create a poem. Share the results with the whole group.

Theater games

Young people and adults are not always conscious of all the tensions that we experience in relationships. We often remain so deeply embedded in our habits of life that we require a range of strategies for surfacing them. We often consider our relationships in the world perfectly normal and fail to problematize, for example, the ways we relate to others — waitresses, shopkeepers, classmates, fellow employees, or the environment. Theater games offer one way of encouraging young people to become more conscious of the patterns by which they relate to the world and how their relationships subsequently affect their hearts. Put differently, theater games help surface the ways young people take external social structures and internalize them deep within their bodies. Once youth have surfaced these habits, even partially, they can consider them in critical and constructive fashion.

Improvisation

One theater game that can prove important for surfacing young people's deep fears, hopes, and dreams is improvisation. Improvisation or "improv" has been used in acting schools for decades as a way of helping actors to surface emotions hidden in their memories in order to better develop their range of emotion. Improvisation offers important techniques for awakening young people to their feelings about the world in which they live: their homes, work, school, regions, nations, and the globe.

1. Organize the youth into small groups of three or four people.
2. Ask each group to improvise a skit in which they depict one memorable situation where they felt a powerful feeling such as anger, sadness, vitality, or joy. Youth may draw from memories of or experiences at church, home, school, work, peer relationships, and so forth.
3. After each group performs, ask the larger group these questions: "What is happening here?" "What was each person feeling?" "Does this situation remind you of anything you have seen here in this church? at home? at school?"
4. To conclude, engage the youth in distilling the theme of the skit by (a) identifying the emotion being depicted, (b) identifying the

situation, for example, "parents angry over youth talking in the church balcony." Discuss how listening to their emotions and being in touch with their heart is part of discernment and is a gift from God that gives them energy to make the world a better place.

5. As a youth minister, keep a list of what occurrences, remarks, or situations that surface in the games make youth push past their apathy to frustration, anger, sadness, joy, love, appreciation, or satisfaction. Make note of the themes and situations around which the group has the most emotion, that is, themes that spark the most intense conversation, highest volume level, or amount of participation. These notes will help you shape your unique youth ministry in your given place.

Body Sculptures

1. Break into groups of three with an "A," a "B," and a "C" player in each group.

2. Describe a situation to be sculpted that includes a barrier to an ideal outcome — for example, a parent with a particular vocational interest for his or her child, an employer exploiting the work of a youth, a teacher assigning arbitrary busy work to a class, and so forth.

3. Player A goes first. Player A "sculpts" — arranges players B and C in particular positions — to create an image of the situation to be depicted. Players B and C remain frozen as others in the larger group observe each sculpture. Ask the observers to discuss what they see and to talk about the emotions they feel.

4. As time goes on, rotate the "sculptor" role to players B and C and ask the young people to choose the situation they want to sculpt. Encourage them to describe personal or structural conflicts, specific or general adolescent tensions, pressures they feel, or other aspects of wherever their imaginations lead them.

Variation: Ask the sculptures to animate in slow motion. Each character moves toward the goal that they seek. Different characters want different things, and so the conflict ensues. Compare the sculptures created by the small groups and ask what they have in common or what is different about them.

Machine of Images

This game requires that a group of youth gather in a circle. The facilitator announces that they will build a machine around a particular theme. The facilitator will have selected a theme previously identified by youth as one around which they have a lot of passion — for example, themes of school, family life, church life, or youth group. The facilitator may say, "We are going to build a machine that represents (your school)." The game begins as members take their places one by one in the middle of the circle to add to the machine. Each person attempts to construct one part of a machine that illustrates their experience of the theme, and each represents their part of the machine using only sound and rhythmic motion with no spoken words. Making matters more challenging — and more fun — each person must also place their body in relation to the other machine "parts" already in place. Placing the parts of the machine in relation to others helps youth see more vividly the reality of systems and how they relate to them. After everyone has taken their place in the machine, the facilitator asks everyone to freeze, and then to slowly look around at the other images and the whole machine. The group is then asked to relax and describe what they are seeing. Every dimension of the machine will quickly appear significant, even the ways the bodies are facing, the horizontal and vertical relationships, and the distance between characters. Finally, the facilitator asks each person to say a word about his or her character and the reasons for representing that character in a particular fashion. This game opens great conversations about particular contexts of adolescent life and young people's feelings about them.

Team survey

The team survey should be undertaken by perceptive youth who can bracket their own biases and view youth in their community as a culture to be investigated. The survey group spends time outside of youth group meetings listening to the informal and unstructured conversations of youth, particularly those times when young people are not saying what is expected of them, but simply talking about what most concerns or excites them.

First, the survey team should identify several contexts in which youth can be observed in casual conversation. Such a list might include coffee rooms, hallways, classrooms, at home, at work, at the park, malls, and before and after worship or church meetings. The survey team should visit these locations and listen to and record in writing the words and actions of the youth passing near. They should keep in mind that young people's conversations reveal various emotional energies, but also deeply held commitments, expectations, and values. The survey team should observe and record the answers to the following questions:

What do youth do?

Who does what?

What are the customs?

Which issues arouse the most emotional interest at present?

What are the most frequent words or phrases used in community discussions?

Following a several-week-long period of observation and recording, the team should prepare a presentation for the youth group that explains and describes their research and facilitates a conversation about young people's commitments, expectations, and values. The youth minister and survey team should carefully attend to the issues that generate enough energy to break through apathy and stimulate initiative in youth.

Video resources

A youth survey team might also use video cameras as a survey tool. Some youth will not mind having cameras observe them in casual moments out of youth group. Be sure that team members understand that they must first seek permission before recording the conversations and actions of others. Videotaped segments of people interacting and conversing can provide helpful resources for groups seeking to identify emotional energies, values, or commitments of a church. Groups of youth may then watch segments together and identify how actions or words display various emotions. For example, one group videotaped a church dinner and observed that while adults sat in one half of the room, youth sat at the far end of the room with each other, which sparked a discussion and further investigation around the theme of youth/adult alienation.

Contemplative practices

Prayer in its many forms has long constituted an important and readily accessible resource for Christians. Prayer creates a rare opportunity for gaining distance from the preoccupations of daily life with all its chatter and diffusions of attention. Prayer creates a space of silence and solitude in which the deep tensions that bind us can be felt, and also in which we can get a clear sense of the grace of the Holy. Those who pray regularly report that in prayer they sometimes experience a flood of emotion around a particular situation that comes to mind. These feelings are more reliable than those experienced in the flow of life's demands. Furthermore, through prayer many people express a deepening appreciation of the Holy, as they are drawn to and transformed by the beauty of God. A few prayer exercises follow.

Centering Prayer

1. Choose a sacred word as the symbol of your intention to consent to God's presence and action within. Examples: Lord, Jesus, Abba, Father, Mother.

2. Sit comfortably with eyes closed and silently introduce the sacred word as the symbol of your consent to God's presence and action within.

   a. By "sit comfortably" I mean relatively comfortably; not so comfortably that you encourage sleep, but sitting easily enough to avoid thinking about the discomfort of your bodies during this time of prayer.

   b. Whatever sitting position you choose, keep your back straight.

   c. If you fall asleep, continue the prayer for a few minutes upon awakening.

   d. Praying in this way after a main meal encourages drowsiness. It is better to wait at least an hour after eating before introducing centering prayer.

   e. We close our eyes to let go of what is going on around and within us.

   f. We introduce the sacred word inwardly and as gently as laying a feather on a piece of absorbent cotton.

3. When you become aware of thoughts, return gently to the sacred word.

   a. "Thoughts" is an umbrella term for every perception, including sense perceptions, feelings, images, memories, reflections, and commentaries.

   b. Thoughts are a normal part of centering prayer.

   c. By "return gently to the sacred word," I mean to suggest that a minimum of mental effort should be used. This is the only activity we initiate during the time of centering prayer.

4. During the course of our prayer, the sacred word may become vague or even disappear.

   a. At the end of the prayer period, remain in silence with eyes closed for a couple of minutes.

b. If this prayer is done in a group, the leader may slowly recite the Lord's Prayer during the additional two or three minutes, while the others listen.

c. The additional two or three minutes give the psyche time to readjust to the external senses and enable us to bring the atmosphere of silence into daily life.

5. Some practical points about centering prayer include:

a. The minimum time for centering prayer is twenty minutes. Two periods are recommended each day, one first thing in the morning, and one in the afternoon or early evening.

b. The end of the prayer period can be indicated by a timer, providing it does not have an audible tick while it is running or a loud sound when it goes off.

c. Physical symptoms:

 – You may notice slight pains, itches, or twitches in various parts of the body or a generalized restlessness. These usually result from the untying of emotional knots in the body.

 – You may also notice heaviness or lightness in the extremities, usually because of a deep level of spiritual attentiveness.

In either case, pay no attention, allow the mind to rest briefly in the sensation, and then return to the sacred word.

While centering prayer is not in itself designed to surface themes or emotions, I have found that the recurring thoughts or distractions that come to mind during the prayer often represent my life situations and my emotional investment in them. Teaching young people to use centering prayer can help them surface their own themes and emotions, and you can use centering prayer as an important part of your youth group's life together.

Focusing Prayer

1. Sit comfortably with your eyes closed. Let your awareness move down into the center of your body and notice what you feel there.

2. Call to mind an experience of desolation (or consolation).

3. Ask yourself if you want to listen to this part of yourself right now. If not, care for the feeling of not wanting to spend time with this thought or image for right now.

4. If it is okay to spend some time with this area of your life, take a few moments to create a loving atmosphere in your mind and body so that it is safe for your feelings to "speak" to you.

5. Notice how your desolation or consolation feels inside you. Where in your body do you especially experience it? Perhaps you feel an ache in your chest, a lump in your throat, a knot in your stomach, or a shaking in your legs.

6. Care for this feeling and see if it wants to tell you about itself, perhaps through a word, an image, or a symbol. Perhaps it wants to come to you as a little child. Perhaps it wants to tell you its name, its history (when and how it developed), and what it needs. (It is often in this part of the prayer practice that we can begin to identify emotions and their source in various situations. These can be generative themes for further reflection.)

7. Whatever feeling comes, reach out to care for it without trying to change it or fix it. You may want to just put a caring hand on the part of your body that is experiencing the feeling. If you wish, ask Jesus, God as you understand God, or some other trusted person to come and help you care for this feeling.

8. Tell this part of you that you will come back at another time and listen to it some more.

9. Before concluding, notice how your body feels as compared to when you began. Are you now carrying this issue differently in your body?

Practicing focusing prayer with youth can raise some very strong emotions. Be prepared to follow up with young people who may need additional attention.

Ignatian Examen

Assumptions that ground the Ignatian practice include the following:

1. God speaks through our deepest feelings.
2. Consolation connects us with ourselves, God, others, the universe. Desolation is whatever disconnects us.
3. Revelation is not over or finished. God is still revealing God's self to us through our experience.
4. Each of us stands uniquely gifted to give and receive love.
5. The Examen helps us to know ourselves, and to stand firm in the face of countervailing forces.
6. We must honor feelings, even those of desolation, in order to hear the story behind them.
7. We can discover the roots of sin by looking at the beginning, middle, and end of any temptation.

The questions of the Ignatian Examen are:

1. For what moment today am I most grateful?
   a. When did I give and receive the most love today?
   b. When did I feel most alive today?
   c. When today did I have the greatest sense of belonging to others, God, the universe, and myself?
   d. When was I happiest today?
   e. What was today's high point?
   f. What gives me life as I face the future?

2. For what moment today am I least grateful?
   a. When did I give and receive the least love today?
   b. When did I most feel life draining out of me?

    c. When did I have the least sense of belonging?

    d. When was I saddest?

    e. What was today's low point?

    f. What do I fear will take life in the future?

Invite young people to join you in the Examen process:

1. Light a candle, take a few deep breaths, place your feet flat on the floor, breath in unconditional love from your toes, feet, legs, abdomen, chest, and throughout your body. As you breathe out, spread this unconditional love to the air around you.

2. Place your hand on your heart and ask God to bring to your heart the moment for which you are most grateful. Reflect upon what was done or said that made it so special. Breathe in gratitude and receive light from that moment.

3. Ask God to bring to your heart the moment for which you are least grateful. Reflect upon what made it so difficult. Be with whatever you feel without trying to fix or change it.

4. Give thanks for whatever you experienced.

5. Share these moments if possible with one other person in the group or with a friend.

The basic reason for using the Examen is that what we speak about becomes more real and important for us and deepens group empathy for one another. In such an environment, people can grow and heal. You can use the Examen after meetings, meals, conversations, and movies; over an entire day or week; on ethnic feast days; at retreats, and so on.

One story of listening

It is often difficult to gain a sense of how listening works apart from seeing how it is embodied in practice. This is the story of how several groups of young people engaged in listening practices to surface generative themes for exploration.

In the summers of 1998 to 2001, as a part of the Youth Discipleship Project, groups of youth from around the country joined together in Claremont, California, and engaged in the listening practices of discernment. Each year, to perceive the most generative energies of their life contexts, the group of sixty youth was divided into smaller groups of twelve youth, each with one adult facilitator.

One particular group surfaced their generative themes through conversation and timed writing. An urgent theme surfaced over several days in which an adult asked participants to respond to several questions:

- When in your life have you felt angry?
- When in your life have you felt sad?
- Where in your life have you felt life draining from you?

These questions were the topic assigned for timed writing exercises and also for many conversations among the group. Among this group were young African American men who had suffered recent tensions with their local police departments. Some had been stopped by local police for "driving while black" or found themselves subject to random searches by police; still others frequently experienced other forms of harassment, including unwarranted suspicion by local shopkeepers: others had experience within the juvenile justice system. Some of these young men felt anger and frustration at their treatment by the police. They felt disturbed by the ways in which the justice systems they encountered viewed them as less than human. The theme explored by this group was, "Some African American males are angry due to unfair treatment in the juvenile justice system."

The emotion around this theme was enormous; every time the topic came up, everyone began talking at once. There was great anger and confusion expressed. The group drew pictures depicting their particular situations. They created small dramatic vignettes as a way of giving concrete shape to the theme, to communicate to each other and the leaders something of the conditions and context for their emotions. This activity allowed the group to gain great clarity about the situations they wished to problematize. As a group they spent the next few weeks exploring the relationships of youth to the law enforcement and justice systems, including recidivism rates, local initiatives for criminalizing normal youth behavior, and the many other ways that urban adolescent life is increasingly constrained. By acting on the heart themes they had surfaced, the young people were empowered in their natural vocations for seeing wrong and working to set it right; they were empowered to their vocations as youth.

The internal goods of listening

One aim of listening for the passions of youth entails discerning where God is working and participating more fully in the transformation of all life for the reign of God. However, viewing listening only as a means of a larger aim risks not understanding the important role of listening as a healing practice with internal goods, even apart from a full-blown discernment process with ultimate aims. In a recent summer program sponsored by the Youth Theological Initiative[6] at Emory University, sixty youth from around the country gathered to engage in practical forms of Christian discipleship and an elaborate program of study, worship, recreation, music, service, and spiritual direction. To the surprise of the staff the activity that consistently ranked highest on youth evaluations was a one-hour interview with a graduate student for research she was gathering. These interviews were very open-ended and allowed youth to speak about feelings and thoughts they had never spoken about to anyone. These researchers found that creating space for these youth to speak did not simply represent an opportunity for them to say what they knew, but in the process of speaking, they found themselves actively making sense of their lives, speaking themselves into identity. Rarely in this culture do youth experience the full and prolonged attention of a significant adult who wants simply to listen *to them* — to hear about their loves, hates, gifts, families, hopes, and dreams for the future. Creating such space for listening to youth is vital for them and for us.

The first movement of practicing discernment with youth is to listen. In that listening you will hear the heart of young people, and together you will both begin to imagine and create your ministry of loving God ... with your heart.

Notes

1. Grace Palladino, *Teenagers: An American History* (New York: Basic Books, 1997), 41ff.

2. Frederick Buechner, *Wishful Thinking: A Theological ABC* (New York: Harper & Row, 1973), 119.

3. For example, "The LORD saw how great man's wickedness on the earth had become, and that every inclination of the thoughts of his heart was only evil all the time" (Gen. 6:5). "Then the LORD said to Moses, "Pharaoh's heart is unyielding; he refuses to let the people go" (Exod. 7:14). "Do not be afraid," Samuel replied. "You have done all this evil; yet do not turn away from the LORD, but serve the LORD with all your heart" (1 Sam. 12:20). "But I trust in your unfailing love; my heart rejoices in your salvation" (Ps. 13:5). "These people honor me with their lips, but their hearts are far from me" (Matt. 15:8). "Love the Lord your God with all your heart and with all your soul and with all your strength and with all your mind and, Love your neighbor as yourself" (Luke 10:27).

4. Walter Brueggemann, *The Prophetic Imagination* (Minneapolis: Fortress Press, 2001), 20.

5. This idea is foundational to Thomas Aquinas's theological system as found in *Summa Theologica*, trans. Fathers of the English Dominican Province (Allen, Tex.: Thomas More Publishing, 1981).

6. For more information on the Youth Theological Initiative, see the Web site http://candler.emory.edu/RESOURCES/YTI.

Five

Understanding

Loving God with your mind —

Movement two

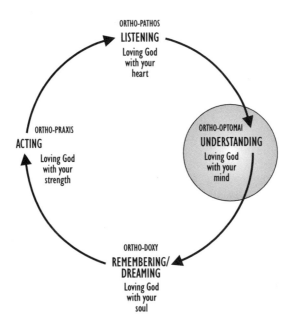

"I hope you will all be able to attend youth group tonight at 7:00 p.m. We are going to study poverty in the United States. We have a panel of experts speaking on the physiological effects and the economic and the political causes of poverty. I think it will be very stimulating and may help us extend our faith," announced the youth minister, Tommy Greer, as he concluded the senior high Sunday school session. "Thanks for coming this morning. I'll see you tonight."

"Poverty...what a downer," whispered Elizabeth Phelps to her friend Susan as they filed out of the classroom.

114

"Yeah...that should be a blast," she responded with her famous sarcasm. "I mean...physiology...economics...politics? Is this school or something?" Susan added.

"I don't know about you," Elizabeth said as she turned to her friend, "but I spend all week long in a boring classroom, and I don't come here to exhaust my brain studying. I come here to get away from school. Am I right?"

Susan nodded in agreement. "And anyway, what's to know about poverty? Some people work hard in school, get good jobs, and make lots of money, while other people don't work hard and end up poor."

Versions of the above scene are repeated in churches across the United States. Many youth workers in recent years have noted a resistance in youth to using their intellects beyond the requirements of schoolwork. In response, some youth leaders simply abandon attempts to engage the intellects of young people, resorting instead to entertaining them. Others try combining entertainment with intellectual content — fitting studies into odd moments of ski trips or lock-ins — in a sort of bait-and-switch strategy. Most conclude that young people's aversion to learning is a normal part of adolescence and should be of no great concern.

Youth's alienation from their intellect, however, is not natural or normal, but is a result of situating young people within educational and commercial structures that drain them of their intrinsic intellectual interest. This chapter explores some of the causes of such alienation among young people and, through historical accounts, suggests that such alienation is not natural or normal. If such alienation from their intellects is not natural or normal, then neither is it faithful. In this chapter I also explore some theological clues for using one's mind in understanding the world. Finally, I suggest some practical ways of engaging youth groups in understanding their worlds.

History bears witness that young people have, at times and places, used their minds in seeking to understand the workings of the world, as a means of attaining roles of greater significance in their communities, and as a source of great delight. In *The Underground History of*

American Education, John Taylor Gatto argues that in this century an aversion to learning has been cultivated among American adolescents, particularly in the system of schooling.[1] He provides numerous examples of young people in early American history who lacked formal education but who, led only by their hunger to learn about their world, became empowered to act on behalf of the common good. For example, Benjamin Franklin left school at age ten, and yet as a writer, politician, scientist, and businessman had few equals among the educated of his day. At an age equivalent to American junior high youth, Franklin read *Pilgrim's Progress,* R. Burton's historical collections (all fifty of them), Plutarch's *Lives,* Defoe's *Essay on Projects,* and Dr. Mather's *Essays to Do Good.*[2] Thomas Edison too left school early because teachers thought him feebleminded. Edison went to work on a train at age twelve, and by the age of thirteen he had set up his own newspaper, which became a main conduit of news during the Civil War. Gatto reminds us that the men who won the American Revolution were barely beyond high school age — Alexander Hamilton was twenty; Aaron Burr, twenty-one; Light Horse Harry Lee, twenty-one; Jean Lafayette, nineteen. Gatto states, "What amounted to a college class rose up and struck down the British empire, afterwards helping to write the most sophisticated documents in modern history."[3] He insists that these examples are not exceptions, but illustrate a norm of educated and empowered young people in early America. Their intelligence was born of a natural hunger for knowledge and the desire to build a radically new kind of nation — rather than the artificial requirements of obtaining a passing grade. Such hunger is natural in young people until it is suppressed by other forces. Gatto argues that many high schools in America today fail to engage this natural curiosity in youth. Such engagement would involve active exploration of the world around them, and invite questioning and creativity in response. High schools that view teaching and learning as imposing an abstract body of knowledge — without evident or felt relationship to youth or their concerns or merely as a means to future employment — do little to engage young people in the delights of learning that can sustain them as agents of faith in this complex world.

Some attribute the weakening of curiosity and intelligence to the exploitation of youth by the entertainment industry. Robert McChesney in the PBS *Frontline* documentary "Merchants of Cool" explains that with dozens of new cable channels competing for viewers and advertising dollars, producers rely on sex and violence as tried and true strategies for getting viewers' attention.[4] With only scant seconds to grab the attention of channel-surfing viewers with remote controls in hand, programmers have no time to develop intricate plots or establish complex characters that would challenge the minds of viewers. Even broadcast journalism has been impacted by the competition of the marketplace, and major network news increasingly resembles the once-disparaged tabloid media, rife with sensational stories ("If it bleeds, it leads!") and superficial analysis.

In this environment, not only is it more difficult to be informed about complex world or local events, but such inattention to complexity becomes a habit of the mind among American youth and adults. As noted by Neal Postman and Marshall McLuhan, our very consciousness is shaped by the expectation of titillation.[5] When we allow ourselves to be so shaped as consumers — judging everything on the basis of whether it entertains us — we forget what it is like to critically explore the world. When we are held captive by entertainment, we suppress our innate curiosity and forget the delights of intellectual endeavor. When youth become targets of media exploitation, their attitudes toward learning are distorted.

Combine this habit of mind forged in a culture of entertainment with the prevailing approaches of education in America that often fail to make learning relevant, and we see more clearly why young people eschew learning in our churches. The love of learning that Franklin, Edison, and countless other early Americans experienced has never been awakened in many youth.

Sadly, many churches capitulate to youth's alienation from their intellects by portraying a simplistic gospel as an easily consumable product that does not require our best thinking. In many churches, the gospel is merely stapled onto the edge of an unreflective consumer life, never allowed to challenge our lifestyles or to, so to speak, "consume us." And yet a thread runs through Christian tradition that calls us to love God with our minds.

Wisdom spirituality

There has existed since before the Christian church a spiritual tradition in the Wisdom writings of the Old Testament which gives priority to exploring with the mind. Old Testament writers revere three types of authoritative literature, representing somewhat distinctive traditions: the Torah, the Prophets, and the Wisdom writings. The Torah is represented in the foundational stories that ground our understanding of a unique God and God's covenant with the people of Israel. The Prophets are situated within these foundational stories, laws, and covenant, but point to the inevitable gaps that become evident between God's promises and the life of particular communities. The Wisdom tradition as embodied in Job, Psalms, Proverbs, Ecclesiastes, and Song of Solomon is a third way of spirituality based on discovery of the world. In Wisdom writings, we have neither the *disclosure* of foundational stories of the Torah nor the *disruption* of status quo in proclamations of the prophets, but instead Wisdom writings disclose a mode of *discernment*. In Proverbs, for example, there is a clear conviction that there is sense, order, and meaning to life — a logos that is both hidden and revealed. In this tradition, the world is not neutral or accidental, not passive, but has regularity, reliability, and recurrence, which permit limited control. Education is the cat-and-mouse game of discovering the order and meaning of the world. The appropriate way to knowledge in this mode is engagement with the world by the reasoning and "meaning-making" mind. According to Walter Brueggemann, "this requires fascination, imagination, patience, attentiveness to detail, and finally, observation of the regularities which seem to govern."[6] Such wisdom cannot be dogmatic, but as it tries to take into account all available experience, it also knows that new experience may cause revision. This form of faith is the root of scientific knowledge, and assumes that knowing how the world works is a good thing. Knowing becomes a human enterprise, but with a clear testimony that there is one who governs this life-giving process in God's own inscrutable pleasure. The wisdom teachers affirm that human experience bespeaks God's gracious mystery.[7] The wisdom teachers have trust that new insights will not lead to a conclusion that life is disconnected, but will lead to new depths of interconnectedness, for the world is one and God is Lord of it all. All exploration moves toward a sense of coherence. Wisdom teachers are on their way (never arriving) to discerning the rationality, the logos, the enduring ordering of reality which is God-given and which endures in the face of every assault and every discontinuity.[8] The discovery of a God-given reality also includes discovery and analysis of threats to this order — in order that they be avoided and challenged.

The incarnational mission of Jesus

Not only did wisdom writings affirm the importance of the mind, but in the incarnation of God in Jesus the mind was an important means of grasping the texture of earthly life and particular situations. Jesus, by enjoining humanity, pointed not to God's salvation from history, but to God's salvation of history — to God's workings amid the particularities of history. In other words, Jesus did not tread lightly on this earth, suspended between heaven and earth, but set his footprints deeply into the earth, among the oppressed, suffering, and sick. In the Apostles' Creed we affirm that "Jesus descended into hell." By one interpretation, this is a way of saying that God was clothed in humanity with all of its suffering. In other words, it pleases God to reconcile the world, not from a distance, but in human form, his heart and body broken by concrete suffering in the world. If human suffering is historically conditioned, so must salvation involve understanding how life is distorted and how it can be reconciled.

Jesus's ministry can be characterized as a ministry among the poor, widows, lepers, imprisoned, blind, the least, and the lost — suffering within a particular historical context, exploited by structural powers and principalities. As suggested by Walter Wink, Jesus's Sermon on the Mount was a response to particular social structures that involved Roman occupation and institutional religion. "If a man strikes you on the right cheek ... if he asks for your coat ... if a soldier asks you to carry his pack one mile ... " were all responses to the abuses of the Roman military and religious leaders of his day. Jesus responded amid the social powers of his world: Roman military occupation, Roman economic extortion of the poor, professional religious leaders who jealously guarded their power, marginalization of women and demonization of the poor, sick, and other victims. The plights of those suffering did not result solely from their personal decisions, but from concentrations of power that gave individuals less power over their own lives. Furthering God's project of love in the world required Jesus to consider love's relationship to these structures that distort and destroy human life. Jesus used his mind to analyze distorted social contexts, and he called for complex responses that expressed a truth beyond social conventions that called for retaliatory violence. Authentic Christian faith never takes us out of the world, but draws us ever further into the world to participate with God in reconciling the broken world. While the heart may be a primary way of knowing God and neighbor, the mind was for Jesus and is for us important for understanding the world's distortions and seeking ways to extend love more completely into the world, to heal its wounds.

Love God in how you put things together

Jesus's love, in addition to requiring analysis of the powers and principalities, also affirms the importance of making sense of discrete experiences, of accurately viewing the whole world in relation to its parts. When the Pharisees attempted to lure Jesus into a series of legal traps by raising tricky questions about paying taxes to Caesar or about whose wife would a woman widowed seven times be in heaven, they concluded their inquiry by asking Jesus for a summary of the law. He responded by quoting Deuteronomy 6, the Shema Yisrael, "You know the law. Love the Lord your God with all your heart, and your soul, and your strength." But according to the account from the Gospel of Mark, Jesus added an additional imperative, "Love God with your mind." The Greek word used in this New Testament text for mind is not *nous* but *dianoia,* suggesting not abstract intellectualization, but instead includes the meaning, "Love God by the way you put things together." It has the meaning of coherence — how we make sense of our discrete experiences and endow with them meaning.

How we put the world together, envisioning the parts in relationship to our whole view of the world, is a significant matter of faith. Many activities, such as eating fast food or watching television, taken by themselves, seem innocent enough. Yet when considered in relation to how they use resources of the earth or exploit human labor, or how their habitual use removes us from other relationships important for sustaining just communities, responsible Christian commitments may require limiting or refraining from these activities. It matters more than ever, how we envision the multiple contexts of our lives — familial, communal, commercial, political, global — and their interrelationships. It matters a great deal, for example, whether we view the world as discrete monads or interrelated ecologies of life. We live in a global era in which nations, economies, industries, and social and environmental ecologies have enormous impact on each other. When asked, before his death, which emerging myths are appropriate to the contemporary era, Joseph Campbell suggested the image of the "earth as a body." This metaphor emphasizes the organic interrelatedness of all life on the planet in ways that older Newtonian mechanistic myths do not. Such interdependence calls for a faith that responds intelligently to this awareness of the systems in which we participate. The understandings, through which we view the world, influence how we sense our responsibility to the world.

Despite the Enlightenment detour that abstracted the mind from the body, the mind is a key instrument of incarnation — implicating God's love deeper into the body of the world. Our experiences of the wounds of others that touch our hearts can be extended by use of our minds as we map the influences that create those wounds. We can, by means of our curiosity or the desire of our minds — by grasping the parts and the whole — extend ourselves into the world in ways that open us to the suffering of others.[9] For example, the systematic domestication of youth — including their exploitation by entertainment and fashion industries, the dulling of their critical skills in educational systems, the criminalization of youth in many states — requires deliberate analysis to grasp.

To participate with God's reconciliation of the world we must cultivate habits of seeing the world accurately — in its complexity and with its full potential. As suggested earlier, orthodoxy or right praise is only one dimension of true discipleship. Christian discipleship must also include ortho-opthamai or "right seeing." We cannot afford to ignore the work of our minds in understanding the structures of our world and responding to them in faith.

The practice of understanding

Having grasped some of the reasons that young people are alienated from the use of their minds, and the importance of accurate perceptions of the workings of the world, what are some practical ways of engaging this movement of understanding? In the last chapter, we explored the importance of listening to the heart and practical ways to surface heart themes from the life contexts of youth. The work of this chapter must be viewed as organically related to the work of the listening movement. Unless the task of exploring the world of adolescents is connected to their own intense feelings — of anger, sadness, frustration, joy, love, or connection — it will become too abstract with no more intrinsic interest than much of their schoolwork. The work of understanding must be grounded in energy intense enough to sustain the work of critical and theological reflection. It is crucial to choose a theme around which the whole room "catches fire" — around which youth feel great passion.

The work of understanding seeks to engage youth and adults together in exploring a situation in some depth. There are two important dimensions of this work: analysis and conceptualization, or moving back and forth between the parts of a problem and a view of the whole. When analyzing a theme, we seek particular causes that impact a situation. In conceptualization of a theme, we begin to see how all the parts or causes of a problem add up to a whole system that relates to other systems. Below are some suggestions for engaging a group of youth in understanding or "problematizing" a heart theme, and envisioning its constitutive relationships.

Guiding questions for understanding

Recall that in the last chapter we described a process in which youth and/or their congregations identify situations that limit life or promote life and fullness. The root question that guides the understanding movement of discernment is "What forces and relationships impact the situation we are trying to understand?" The discernment process we are describing here includes focusing reflection around one or a group of situations surfaced in the "listening movement." The more we extend our investigation to include a number of themes, the more likely we are to gain a sense of systems that hold us.

We can break the root question into several specific questions. Any serious attempt to "understand" a situation might include a range of questions, such as:

- Why does the situation exist?
- What forces have aligned in order to allow this situation?
- What individual decisions were made?
- What community decisions were made?
- How do social institutions, expectations, and pressures impact this situation?
- What is the role of economic pressures?
- What is the role of political forces?
- What is the role of cultural forces?
- What is the role of religious expectations, norms, values, and beliefs?

- What is the role of ethnic expectations, norms, values, and beliefs?

- What is the role of human psychology in creating this situation — including deep fears and hopes?

One way we can grasp the complexities of our world and our place in it is by drawing a map. Maps are conceptual frameworks for understanding relationships of distance between cities, rivers, highways, mountains, and so on. This practice of discernment seeks to develop in youth and congregations the skill of mapping various kinds of relations to others in the world, to construct a map of the world of young people and their concerns. Each situation of tension or joy includes many relational dimensions — personal, psychological, social, economic, political, religious, ethnic. Rarely do we step out of the flow of our lives in order to see and understand how we are in relationship to each of these forces, how they impact us and we them. In each of these relationships we find an opportunity to be in partnership with God in the healing of the world, by supporting, resisting, or challenging the relationships that surround and constitute us. We might understand the process of investigating the world as "unraveling." Some find it helpful to think of the world as a woven cloth held together by many threads. While the cloth of our lives may appear seamless, when we pull on these threads one by one we can better see how the garment is constructed, how it holds together.

This process of discernment, of mapping and understanding our world, is best done as a communal process in which we reflect, discuss, and re-create together an increasingly accurate picture of the world and how it works. It is crucial that these conversations include the range of voices and experiences of youth and adults of a particular community, to give a fuller sense of the many sides of the situation. Through these rich discussions youth and adults create common visions of their world, enhancing their perspective on the world. Some of the images constructed in these conversations will support dominant visions of the world, while others will challenge them.

Youth and adults can become lively co-investigators of their world when these processes are done well. For many youth this process represents a first opportunity to reflect upon their lives, not simply flowing with these forces, but investigating them. Some feel a palpable excitement in using their minds. Others discover something important about a collaborative process in which many engage in telling the story of their experience. Still others are comforted by the realization that their experiences of the world are not solitary, but are shared by others. And for yet others, something even more vital emerges about the prospects of partnership with God in the world's transformation. This process of coming to understand, map, or unravel the situations of limit or fullness in our world can be broken down into several steps.

The steps to understanding

Step 1: Observing and describing

Understanding situations of limit and fullness requires deliberately *observing and describing* the specific concrete situations that evoke these emotions. Those seeking to participate with God must understand the present action of their community and name the present circumstances evoking particular emotions. Until we can understand the dynamics of "what is going on," we cannot see beyond to further possibilities. We must ask, "What is going on here?" "What is being done here?"

Step 2: Reflecting critically

Understanding a situation also means raising questions about the social and personal dynamics as shaped by economic, political, and cultural forces. We rarely find cultures, traditions, or social influences in any pure state, but rather they mingle with multiple other ethnic, class, religious, or pop cultural traditions. The appropriate questions for these understanding activities are "But why?" "What are the reasons that this situation has emerged in history?" "What are all of the influences upon this situation?" As we attend to our emotions, reflect upon them and the situations in which they are evoked, make judgments about them, and act faithfully in ways that honor them, we can participate in the transformation and healing of the world.

Step 3: Back and forth between the part and the whole

While focusing on each issue alone may be helpful in some ways, we risk addressing problems at a superficial level if we do not seek to gain a sense of the larger systems. In order to foster this sense of the whole we must engage youth in focusing directly upon one small dimension of their lives — one tension or one joy. But periodically we must engage them in grasping the gestalt of their social reality to determine how the parts relate to the whole. By moving back and forth between the parts and the whole we find that youth and congregations weave together an increasingly accurate picture of the relationships that constitute their social world and beyond.

Practical approaches for understanding themes

Clearness committees

Through the centuries, Christians have refined practices of making good decisions. In the Quaker tradition, anyone seeking to make good decisions may call together a group of church members and friends to help them consider a decision. The meeting of this group, which is called a *clearness committee,* begins and ends with silence, maintaining a spirit of openness and prayerful waiting. The four to ten members of the committee simply ask questions of the person seeking clarity to help surface issues, concerns, and understandings that may help them. The committee does not expect that each problem will have an answer or response, but expects instead to give the seeker a community of support and a frame of reference for considering the decision. The clearness committee does not give advice, but focuses on the person requesting clearness.

A youth group may organize a clearness committee to explore a generative theme. A committee may raise questions about the causes and relationships of a particular theme in such a way as to give direction to their search. For example, a clearness committee might raise questions about the impact of consumerism on children working in sweatshops in other countries, on our own hearts, our relationships with others, our self-perception. All of these questions might then represent different directions that a group or small groups might explore.

"But why?" method

A simple way to introduce youth to the idea of mapping or problematizing is articulated in the book *Training for Transformation* by Anne Hope et al., and is called the "But why? method."[10] In this method, people are led through a process of how to question a particular situation. Young people might begin with a situation they already have some clarity about. For example, I have frequently used the limit situation, "Rosa Parks's feet hurt." This theme captures a historical situation with many root causes that youth can explore as an exercise. The facilitator probes the group, "Why did Rosa Parks's feet hurt?" The group might respond, "Because she had to give up her seat on the bus in Alabama in 1955." The facilitator might push, "But why did she have to give up her seat?" The group might respond, "Because of the racist policies of the city of Montgomery that required her to sit at the back of the bus." The facilitator might counter, "But why were there racist policies?" The group might say, "Because the folks in power were white and they had a history of seeing black people as inferior." The facilitator might push behind this, "But why did they have a history of seeing black people as inferior?" Depending on their understanding of history, they might respond, "Because they owned slaves to make cotton crops profitable for the South." The conversation might not be linear or include only direct causation, but causes might branch out in many parallel directions, including psychological, ethnic, cultural, economic, political, or religious.

As the group fleshes out the multiple causes for a particular theme in this way, the facilitator may depict the causes in some kind of chart form for all to follow along. The chart develops into a full-blown map of a theme as the group contributes their understandings of the problem, perhaps resulting in a flowchart with arrows and devices to indicate relationships between the causes. In this way, a facilitator can prepare a group for doing this kind of mapping with any theme.

As the group comes to the end of its knowledge of a particular situation, the facilitator should probe the group to get a deeper sense of the root causes for a situation. For example, one of the causes listed for Rosa Parks's feet hurting might include the fact that she just bought new shoes. While one dimension of the causal nexus, her shoes do not constitute a root cause for her suffering. Sometimes the root causes are clear and sometimes not. And often the understanding of the root causes shifts as the group collects more information about the problem. Identifying the root causes for a situation helps a group focus their theological reflection and their action. It would not be as effective for a group to, for example, agree to give up their seats on a bus or to pass laws making it illegal for shops to sell ill-fitting shoes, if the social conditions that contributed to such discrimination continued unchecked.

As a group reflects on causes for a situation, they often reach the limits of their knowledge about the situation. In a sense, this exercise may raise more questions than it answers. It is always best for a group to strain for answers themselves, even when their information is limited. Such strain creates a curiosity for more information, at which time they may request the input of experts. This approach is similar to the way mathematics is taught in some classrooms in Japan, where a teacher gives a class a problem to solve and does not tell them how. The class is left to struggle for the answers using the limited formulas with which they are familiar. After an hour or so, when the class has reached a point of frustration, they are more ready for the teacher to help them with new formulas and methods for solving the problem. Hence the class learns in a way more organically related to their own questions and tensions.

Boal's exercises

Augusto Boal, Brazilian activist, educator, and performer, has explored with great success the use of drama and theater games by communities who wish to problematize their life-world. He assumes that our rational minds are limited in their awareness of how we are present to our daily lives. For example, much as we drive a car without having to think about it, we sleepwalk through much of our lives without being conscious about the ways we participate in either life or death. Boal practices a number of ways of enabling people to surface the felt experiences of their lives, to make them conscious in order to become objects of their reflection. His theater games have been useful in surfacing unconscious experiences of racism, oppression, and injustice.

For many youth, the activities involved in analysis can be tedious and dry. But Boal's use of drama helps young people reflect upon social structures and relationships in a way that is energizing rather than draining, drawing upon the primary sources of their own experience in the world.[11]

Professions

In Boal's game "Professions," each player receives a piece of paper with the name of a profession on it — doctor, lawyer, prostitute, bartender, teacher, and so on. When the facilitator gives a signal, all actors start playing their professions at the same time, with actions and sounds but no words. As they perform they should seek to illuminate as many details about the activities of the profession as they can. To help this evolve as a game, the facilitator should ask them to find others who have something in common with themselves. As the actors form groups of four or five, depending upon how they conceive of commonalities, they will stand together in the room. At some point the facilitator asks each group to come to the front of the room and perform their actions. Still without words, observers in the room are asked if they can guess what the portrayals of professions have in common. People make connections that those depicting the professions and forming common groupings never imagined. The conversations that emerge around commonalities are a form of reflection on the ways professions are situated in relation to each other: how the businessman relates to the prostitute, how the teacher relates to the principal, how the doctor relates to the lawyer, and so on. Each group performs the actions of their professions as observers guess and discuss the commonalities. You can make this game more relevant when the professions are related to the themes that young people are investigating. For example, if the theme is related to the frustration of youth in high schools, then the professions might include the roles of student, teacher, principal, and parents.

Image Theater

Boal utilizes images to freeze social situations that are pregnant with emotional energy and multiple relationships. For example, young people might be invited to create a machine — either a frozen image or a machine with interrelated moving parts. For example, the machine for the theme "high school" might contain images of young people struggling, teachers frustrated, principals wielding power, or parents crying. Such a machine might also include an image of a corporation standing outside of the school machine symbolizing some set of expectations or pressures felt in the high school. Youth may be invited to join the machine one by one, to contribute some dimension that represents their experience of the truth of the theme. By allowing the machine to have moving parts, youth are allowed to more fully represent relationships and their interaction. For example, a teacher making a violent pointing action toward youth contains much symbolic meaning. When fifteen or twenty young people have joined the machine, they have created something resembling the true situation of the theme under consideration. Another dynamization of the machine might include allowing each actor to say one phrase that captures the essence of their relationship to the whole: "I'm so tired of your behavior!" "I don't understand why we have to do this assignment!" "Why can't you teach our children?" Such a machine has the potential for making young people more conscious of social relationships.

Drawings

I once participated with a group of Los Angeles day laborers who were trying to raise the awareness of other laborers and employers about their community. A small and ingenious group of Mexican day laborers drew a beautiful four-by-four-foot picture depicting the different neighborhoods of their city. They had drawn police stations, parks, schools, factories, retail stores, bus stops, and suburban neighborhoods. The drawing was not inflammatory, but accurately depicted the way the city was laid out. The men invited a group composed of laborers and employers to simply walk around the drawing and make notes about what they saw. After almost an hour of observing the very rich painting, the participants were asked to contribute their insights. For almost another hour, laborers and employers made connection after connection identifying things they had never seen before — inequities in bus routes, placement of police stations, the dearth of parks in urban neighborhoods where workers lived, the distance between the urban apartments of the workers and the suburban homes of the employers, and so forth. The employers gained a different sense of what the workers' lives must be like. They also came to understand the injustice of public policies in their area. They came to understand in a more real way their need for each other, the necessity of forming coalitions together, and significantly, of the employers providing more just wages and conditions for the workers. With such drawings young people can reflect upon their social location in relation to, for example, schools, entertainment markets, service sector employment, and family pressures.

Debate

One way of drawing young people deeper into analysis is to stage a debate with youth representing opposite sides of a topic. Their desire to make a good showing in the debate often prompts research and analysis that may not happen otherwise. For example, a debate on abortion may surface many statistics, book citations, and pastoral and parental opinions. While debates may use these resources and engage a community in working toward constructing a common perspective, you want to avoid polarizing youth on different sides of an issue. Facilitators must seek ways for young people to hold their opinions loosely and yield them when necessary — in moving toward consensus.

Codes and decoding

Paulo Freire went into poor communities and made drawings and took photographs of various situations within which people lived. He took photos of people growing crops, taking grain to sell to the co-op, washing clothes in a stream, and walking to work or school. He showed these to small groups of citizens and asked, "What do you see? What is happening here? What are they feeling? What is your experience of this? Does this happen in your community?" Freire observed that some photos would be discussed matter of factly, while others would generate much emotion and energy. Freire learned that the pictures which generated energy or caused everyone to talk at once were the most important subjects of focus. In these discussions, Freire learned a great deal about the people's experiences, their relationships with merchants, land owners, factories, and politicians.

In our work at the Claremont School of Theology, we employed Freire's codes with much success among youth and churches. Usually, we were able to discern with some accuracy the situations in the lives of young people that constituted contexts of limit or fullness. Often, these could be depicted through simple drawings. In the same way that Freire showed pictures to small groups of citizens, we showed drawings to groups of youth and adults as a way of stimulating conversation about the situations. For example, one drawing depicted a young girl in her room. Her room was decorated with ballet slippers, ballet trophies, and ballet pictures. From the doorway her father is looking through with a frown on his face. In his hand is an application to the local business school of the university. From his expression, they are clearly in an argument. She is sad, with her head in her hands. He is adamant. This picture generated much discussion about the pressure for young people to be successful in financial terms, the limits our society places on vocation, and the pressures parents feel to be validated by their children's success.

Library or Internet research

Young people can easily explore issues and topics via Internet word searches. For young people who desire a deeper sense of history, background, and statistics around a particular issue, the Internet can be a great resource. The Internet has expanded the options for young people who would not darken the door of a library.

Empirical research

Young people need to generate ideas about ways to explore their world. While, at times, statistical evidence and expert witnesses may be called for, young people remain eager about their learning when it includes their own research, including observation, interview, or other forms of qualitative and quantitative analysis. For example, one group of young people exploring the issue of racism in a local police department developed a questionnaire and went to local shopping malls to ask people of color about their treatment at the hands of the local police. Another group exploring gender stereotypes developed a test in which young women dressed in several various styles, including punk, grunge, promiscuous, preppy. They took their experiment to a local professional baseball game to test the reactions of people to these varying styles of women's clothing. Another group studying abuse in dating relationships enacted a skit in which a young boy spoke abusively to his girlfriend at a local burger stand to see if any of the customers would intervene. They later interviewed the customers to get a better sense of their feelings and reactions.[12]

Keeping charts

Analysis of situations usually surfaces various streams of causes that branch out in all directions. In other words, there is rarely one cause for a particular situation. For example, the Jim Crow laws that created the context for Rosa Parks's discrimination were caused by a variety of factors ranging from Southern traditions rooted in slavery, economic demands of the industrializing North, psychological distortions in the minds of whites, theological distortions promoted among some Christian denominations, and scientific views that distinguished racial types in a hierarchy. Such causes overlap and influence each other in interesting ways. It can be helpful for a group to attempt to chart how causes relate to each other. Causes for situations and themes can be charted in various ways — as flowcharts that flow from the effect downward into many causes, or as a web of interrelated causes that encircle the theme that seems caught in its web of influences. Creating such charts and posting them on the wall of youth groups can serve as important reminders of how current discussions relate to their existential concerns. For example, if youth do not see some direct correlation between their discussion of economics and politics and their consumption of music and movies, they may resist or lose interest in the topic. Making the connections apparent helps to retain interest in topics, keeping them from being irrelevant abstractions.

One story of understanding

In the last chapter, I related a story about a group of youth who, through conversation, timed writing, art, and drama, unearthed a theme common among them, specifically "Some African American males are angry because of unfair treatment in the juvenile justice system." In the weeks that followed the naming of a common theme, this group of twelve young people explored the situation, seeking to understand its causes — the forces that culminate to produce this theme. These young people were asked to envision themselves as detectives seeking clues to a crime.

In their planning together, this team decided first to create an informal survey to administer among young people at malls and schoolyards. The team wanted to determine whether this theme was pervasive or isolated. Although not a scientific survey, their interviews did reveal a trend in their communities. Ethnic minority young people were being singled out by police. Another experiment involved sending two young people — one white, one African American — into local shops to see if they were treated differently.

In the course of exploring issues related to youth and their relationships with police and juvenile justice systems, the young people in this youth group discovered that a local town council was completing an investigation into a routine traffic stop in which a young African American man, who was also an excellent student and beginning college in the fall, was shot by police. The group sat in on several town council meetings in which members of the council and local experts reported statistics regarding the treatment of young black males at the hands of local police. The group took copious notes and created charts on the statistics to report to the entire group.

Additionally, in the course of their investigation, these young people were invited to the offices of the Los Angeles chapter of the ACLU to listen to a report on upcoming legislation threatening to further target minority youth and criminalize juvenile offenses that were previously only misdemeanors. This report helped these young people to flesh out their picture of the situation under consideration.

In addition to their efforts to explore this theme, some youth did Internet searches and compiled statistics on the issues that were surfacing. Finally, on one evening this group of twelve youth created a skit that effectively communicated to the larger group of sixty youth the findings of their research. It is important to note that this movement to understanding did not primarily involve lectures by experts, although some experts were engaged to help flesh out their understandings. These lectures were also about themes and situations with existential interest for these young people.

This group of young people were not only analyzing the particular situations, but beginning to understand the systems — economic, political, cultural — that help to create the context. These young people retained a high degree of interest and indeed, investigation served to intensify their interest, in the subject they were exploring. Having engaged this theme in analysis and conceptualization, they were eager to explore the logic of God in relation to these situations and systems.

The intrinsic goodness of understanding

The second movement of practicing discernment with youth is understanding — loving God with your mind. For much of this chapter I

have articulated the work of the mind in a somewhat utilitarian fashion, as a tool of the heart, as a tool of faithfulness, as a means of
transformation, extending love into the world. Yet, such a view is
not complete without illuminating the work of the mind as satisfying
and healing in its own right. In my work with youth, I have observed
something like delight as young people learn to think — to fall in love
with learning. Young people often find significant healing when they
discover the powers of their minds. Especially in this culture, which
tends to shape young people as passive consumers and in which learning is reduced to the function of securing a future job, our engagement
of young people in playfully exploring the world through disciplined
use of the mind constitutes a significant healing. Many young people
experience a rare moment when learning is embraced for its intrinsic
satisfaction — beyond whatever purposes may be imposed by the necessities of their social context. Theologically stated, engaging young
people in passionate learning is a powerful dimension of their human
vocation.

Notes

1. John Taylor Gatto, *The Underground History of American Education: A
School Teacher's Intimate Investigation into the Problem of Modern Schooling*
(Oxford: Oxford Village Press, 2000).

2. Ibid., 28.

3. Ibid., 25.

4. PBS Video "The Merchants of Cool," original airdate: February 27, 2001.
Produced by Barak Goodman and Rachel Dretzin, directed by Barak Goodman, writ-
ten by Rachel Dretzin, correspondent and consulting producer Douglas Rushkoff. A
FRONTLINE Co-Production with 10/20 Productions, LLC.

5. See, for example, Marshall McLuhan and Quentin Fiore, *The Medium Is
the Massage* (New York: Bantam Books/Random House, 1967); Neil Postman,
Technopoly: The Surrender of Culture to Technology (New York: Vintage Books,
1993), and *Amusing Ourselves to Death: Public Discourse in the Age of Show
Business* (New York: Penguin Books, 1993).

6. Walter Brueggemann, *The Prophetic Imagination* (Minneapolis: Fortress
Press, 2001), 72.

7. Ibid., 83.

8. Ibid., 85.

9. Thomas Aquinas understood the mechanism for our return to God as desire
or passion. He spoke of all creation as having proportionate attractions to those

goods that enhance life and avoidance of others that would diminish life — for example, a rock held above ground is attracted to the earth, fire is attracted to air and not water, which might extinguish it. In important ways, these attractions point to a human longing for God that draws us forward until we rest in God. His name for the mechanisms of this attraction and avoidance was *appetitus,* which he categorized as three — the natural (physical), the sensate (cognitional), and the intellective (rational) *appetitus.* Aquinas associates spiritual reality with freedom. Rocks are constrained by natural laws and are not free, while animals have sensory perceptions and instincts that give them more freedom, but are not free to extend themselves beyond their instincts and senses. Humans have the greatest freedom because we are not determined by laws of physics or instincts alone, but we also have the power to order life through the use of our intellects — including choice and intentionality. According to Aquinas, this human freedom is an important dimension of our spirituality.

The intellect can be thought of as an appetite that pulls us to the good, the true and the beautiful. In other words, intellect itself includes passion, the mind is not content with ignorance, but is restless to understand human relationships and experiences. This passion of the mind also infuses the rest of the composite human creature, the body and the emotions, with intellective and evaluative capacity.

10. Anne Hope, Sally Timmell, and Chris Hodzi, *Training for Transformation: A Handbook for Community Workers,* 4 vols. (Gweru, Zimbabwe: Mambo Press, 1995).

11. Augusto Boal has written several volumes, any of which might be helpful for youth ministers or educators. The one with the most inclusive list of games is *Games of Actors and Non-Actors,* trans. Adrian Jackson (London: Routledge, 1992).

12. This is an approach called invisible theater, developed by Augusto Boal.

Six

Remembering and dreaming

Loving God with your soul—

Movement three

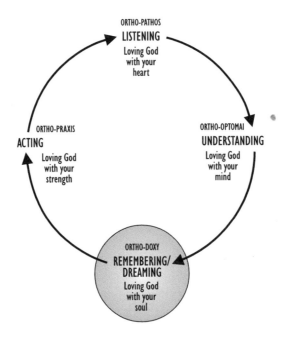

"No, I don't like it, but that's just the way it is!" declared Anna Ramirez when her mother questioned her about her torn shirt. "At school some of the boys try to grope me in the hallways between classes. They try to touch me and they make lewd comments as I pass between them. Sometimes they pin me against the lockers. And not only me, but all the girls," she explained.

"Anna, I'm shocked!" her mother gasped. "I had no idea it was like that at your school."

"It's like that everywhere, Mom. I have friends from other schools who say it is like that at their schools too," said Anna.

"But where are the teachers and the principal when all of this groping is going on?" questioned her mother.

"Oh, they mostly look the other way. Besides, what can they do? Boys are just like that. It's something girls just have to put up with."

This conversation overheard between a mother and her daughter reveals how distorted situations can become normalized in the minds of teens. Without memory of a time when situations were different — when culture did not support such lewdness in boys, when administrators and girls themselves were outraged by such behavior — young people often believe that such is the natural way of things and nothing can be done about it. Today, many young people grow up thinking that a great many dehumanizing situations are normal — for example, expectations of thin, sexualized female bodies; violence as a way of solving problems; gender inequality; racial prejudice; inordinate ambition for status, power, and wealth; and pressures to buy and consume. Without an orientation in Christian faith, many youth do not imagine the possibilities for the world to be different or remember their own yearnings for such a world. Christian faith invites us to re-member our best selves, our souls — our highest hopes and strengths, and to dream of a world that promotes such flourishing among all creatures. The term "soul" has diverse connotations, but is typically qualified by adjectives such as "higher," "deeper," "true," or "best" — pointing to dimensions of our self beyond our immediate or superficial impulses. Living into and from our "soul" or "true self" requires us to engage in practices that help us to resist our superficial responses distorted by cultural pressures or personal hubris, and that draw out the best in us — the life and glory for which we were created.

Our dance with the holy and the dynamics of faith

According to Christian theologians, our souls are vitalized in a dance with God, our holy partner. Yet, this vitalizing dance begins in God's own interior practice. Dancing is an appropriate metaphor for describing the inner life within the Triune personhood of God. In this interior dance of God, the three persons of Father, Son, and Spirit are open to each other, interpenetrating each other, being transformed by mutual relationship — which is love. This interrelationality within the Trinity defines God's primal project of love, which by definition cannot remain closed in upon God's self, but must move outward beyond itself or else it would not be love. God extends this love to creation, inviting us to join the dance that has its source within the Triune God. The Holy Spirit lures us, not by coercion, but through love and beauty, into the dance that leads us ever toward God's reign, awakening us to God's love, empowering us into full humanity, and sending us out to participate with the Spirit in reconciling the whole world in this way of love.

This dance with God involves us wholly — moving us heart, mind, soul, and body toward God and the full life for which we were created. Perhaps the worst of dancers are those who dance from their heads — who memorize the steps from a book or painted numbers on a floor. We simply cannot dance well by our intellects alone. We must yield heart, mind, soul, and body to full relationship with the living God. Although Christians at times flatten out this relational dance or reduce it to a list of doctrines or rules to make it safe and predictable, our best theological and mystical traditions point to a living God who resists such codification, and with whom we respond in our full being. Just as no dance can be reduced to a mere sequence of steps, but requires responsiveness to one's partner, neither can Christian faith flourish without such full openness to God. In this dance with God, we discover a space in which our own dreams of fullness and community come alive and our future opens before us. In this dance we are shaped by God's beauty while the noise and distractions that prevent us from hearing our deep yearnings for God, neighbor, and fullness fade into the distance.

Although our dance with God remains open and spontaneous, we can identify ways of relating to our Partner that promote love, reconciliation, and human flourishing. Just as any dance requires skills that must be practiced in order to be improved, so does our dance with the Holy require practices for attuning to God. For Christians, these practices have included Bible study, prayer, worship, living in community, feasting, fasting, extending hospitality to the stranger, keeping the Sabbath, living simply, and seeking justice. We need not treat practices as rules to keep, but as ways to attune to our Partner and invite others into the dance. These practices move us deeper into the heart of God's reign of fullness and beauty, for which we were created. While it is beyond the scope of this chapter to elaborate all the ways in which Christians have connected their lives with God, in what follows I elaborate two key practices that Christians have found helpful in nurturing memory and dream of this alternate and true reality. Christians have relied upon prayer and theological reflection — *remembering and dreaming* — for connecting with and enlivening their souls.

Remembering: Wholeness through prayer[1]

The situation of youth described in this book acknowledges a broken or "dis-membered" world. A recurring theme in this volume has concerned the awareness of a world in which forces fragment the individual and social wholeness for which we yearn in our souls. We have discussed the fragmentation of our communities, in which adults and young people are alienated from each other and the common good. In our discussion of the "Frankenstein monster" of adolescence, we have also attempted to clarify how young people are alienated from their best selves, their signature gifts, their hearts, minds, souls, and strength. The mechanisms of this fragmentation and alienation are subtle and insidious. They include the busy pace of life, constant entertainment distractions that dissociate young people from themselves and their world, fashion and commodity advertisements that seduce them with glittering promises of fulfillment and happiness, culturally validated ambitions that relentlessly drive individuals onward without care for others, and a host of habits, such as convenience and consumption, that limit our perspectives and obscure the possibilities for the world's reconciliation. Yet this fragmentation and alienation are not the final words on the possibilities for life.

As suggested in the first chapter, the Triune God of Christian faith is characterized by unity in diversity, and God's reign involves the fulfillment of all creation in unity and diversity. The seeds for this wholeness are hidden within each creature and our yearning for fullness and reconciliation. Prayer "re-members" or reconnects us to the memory of our yearning for love and reconciliation with God, neighbor, and ourselves. In prayer, our distractions are muted, and the deeper call of our hearts to love God and neighbor is amplified.

While prayer has taken many forms and purposes through history — including, for example, intercession, supplication, confession, and thanksgiving — all prayer includes a dimension of contemplation. As the term connotes, contemplation involves a habit of seeing more deeply. As suggested by Anthony DeMello, the greatest act of love is not service, but "seeing truly and deeply," into the wounds and blessings hidden beneath our facades or projections. While our culture presents enormous barriers to contemplation — reducing everyone and everything to its utility — prayer creates the space to change how we view God, neighbor, and self. In our silence before the Holy, we hear the cries of our own wounded hearts and those of the world yearning for reconciliation, those muffled by the distractions of contemporary life. As God awakens and enlivens these yearnings within us, we are moved to participate in God's reign, mirroring the unity and diversity of God's own Trinity.

While youth ministers have often sought to introduce young people to the gospel of Jesus through concerts and high-energy events, an overemphasis on spectacle risks drowning out the voice of the soul that calls young people to re-member love and to be reconciled with God and neighbor. If Tom Beaudoin is right that postmodern young people hunger for "experience," this cannot simply include sensationalism, but surely also includes the sensible call of their own hearts to love God and neighbor.[2] Our young friend Anna, whose conversation we overheard at the beginning of the chapter, would find in prayer an important resource for resisting abuse and the expectation that she was meant for no more. To help us practice prayer and contemplation with young people, some practical suggestions appear at the end of this chapter.

Dreaming: The Christian story-formed perspective

The Christian story cultivates an alternate perspective of the world, a dream in which the world is being reconciled. Such a dream should not distract young people from this life and world, but direct their focus on God's work in history and their call to partnership in its healing. As argued in this book, young people inhabit a world that promotes a story about human life and its salvation through consumption, in which other people are objects of our desire — or else obstacles to our own success, in which winning and achieving is best, while losing is to be deplored. The ubiquity of this story makes it difficult to challenge. In order to resist the destructive force of this story, another story needs to be told. While remembering, through prayer, that the deep cries of their hearts are important in resisting forces that inhibit the flourishing of all creatures, the Christian story helps youth to connect their stories to the story of God, giving a context for faith that extends backward to creation and forward to creation's completion. Especially in a commercial culture that obscures history and leaves young people feeling isolated in the cosmos, the Christian story relates them to a great cloud of witnesses.

As acknowledged by many others, including Stephen D. Jones, author of *Faith-Shaping: Youth and the Experience of Faith*,[3] young people grow up biased according to the stories that form them. A neutral environment without bias is not possible, and by failing to orient young people to an alternate story we relegate them to a culture that tells its own stories. In his book *Creative Word*, Walter Brueggemann reveals the important role of the Torah in the faith of Israel, as a paradigm for understanding the importance of grounding Christian faith in foundational stories. Although Brueggemann's focus is on the literature of the Old Testament — the Torah, prophets, and Wisdom writings — his work offers insight into dynamics of faith that culminate in the person of Jesus and Christian faith. Referring to his study at length gives us a sense of the importance of the Christian story as a foundation for forming youth.

The way of the Torah

The people of Israel claimed the Pentateuch, the first five books of the Old Testament, as their primary authority, fundamental for all that would come after them and foundational for education. Brueggemann's focus is not on the specific content of the Torah — the five books of the Pentateuch and the stories contained in them — but on the unique way of knowing represented in them and their role in shaping the identity of Hebrew and Christian people. He suggests that in observing the role of the Torah in these earlier religious communities we gain a sense of the importance of primal stories for all religious communities. Brueggemann writes:

> The Torah is a statement of community ethos, a definitional statement of the character of the community, which is given and is not negotiable among the new generation. In this first part of the canon, it is clear that the community precedes the individual person, that the community begins by stating its parameters and the perceptual field in which the new person must live and grow.[4]

Brueggemann argues that telling and retelling these foundational stories in rituals of remembrance and reflection establish this perceptual field. For the people of Israel, rituals formed the context for teachable moments, not because they functioned as coercive events, but because they offered experiences evoking curiosity among children and youth. Education begins, in other words, as children yearn to belong to the secret. Teaching, in turn, becomes the shrewd management of that secret.[5] Adults respond to the earnest questions of youth by articulating the classical testimonies of faith. The Torah is a gift given with firm graciousness.

The Torah invites members into a story-formed perceptual field or way of seeing the world, God's work, and our role in it — while members of other communities have different stories; this is ours, our identity. The role of the Torah was to provide a way for the community to tell its story in a manner that encompassed all of creation and the entirety of history, together with the very personal promises of God for the particular community. The Torah represents a "pre-doubt world"[6] — a set of stories and concepts that provides a distinctive way of viewing the world and our place in it. While other modes of learning exist that require different hermeneutics which raise questions about relevant interpretations, the stories of the Torah form a context for subsequent practices of suspicion. But the primal stories themselves remain the same and we understand ourselves as continuing the story.

As the Torah was appreciated by Israel, the Christian story in a similar way provides a distinctive manner of viewing the world that can be comprehended across generations. Language is one dimension of religious ethos shaped by our foundational stories. Craig Dykstra illustrates the importance of religious language for youth. He recalls a short story by Flannery O'Connor:

> Two fourteen-year-old girls have taken to calling each other "Temple One" and "Temple Two." ... The source of all this hilarity is a lecture they had recently received at their convent school from the oldest nun, Sister Perpetua, on what to do if a young man should "behave in an ungentlemanly manner with them in the back of an automobile." They were to say: "Stop sir! I am a Temple of the Holy Ghost — and that," according to Sister Perpetua, "would put an end to it."[7]

Dykstra notes that the idea of "Temple of the Holy Ghost," although quaint, may provide these young girls a way of orienting themselves in the Christian story, and their relationships to an ultimate reality and shared way of life.

Drawing on Erik Erikson's work on identity formation, Dykstra observes, "Adolescents invest significant energies in striving to interpret themselves and their world in coherent, meaningful, workable and personally satisfying ways.... They are involved in a search for a way of life, and the process is at once social and linguistic."[8] Language grounded in Christian stories and concepts provides youth with important resources for negotiating identity in a confusing and alienating world. Such a language and perspective could be a gift to Anna, who is locked into a normalized situation without any alternate way of viewing her treatment. We must create an environment, in short, in which Anna can envision herself as part of a movement of God stretching back to creation's beginnings and into a future in which all creation finds fulfillment in God's redemption. The best curriculum for forming youth in this story is to see and experience its embodiment in the corporate life of a vital congregation. A few suggestions for engaging young people in the Christian story and tradition are found at the conclusion of this chapter.

The foundational Christian story provides an important resource for faith and identity, but such a way of knowing does not exhaust the ways God speaks.

The way of the prophets

While the story-formed ethos of the Torah provides a consensus in which a Christian community can orient itself, the prophetic way illuminates another source of our dreams for our lives and the world. While the Torah grounds our identities in a particular story and ethos, we must nevertheless acknowledge the potential for dominant culture to domesticate our stories. There is enormous pressure for religious communities to conform to culture — whether organized around the power of Augustus, Constantine, Hitler, or Madison Avenue. The domestication of religious stories in conformity to political, economic, or cultural forces risks ignoring the wounded of the community and provides the context for the cry of the biblical prophets. In the prophets, Brueggemann states, "we are dealing with the pathos of God and of Israel, with the sense of fracture... between what is at hand and what is promised."[9] The prophets do not merely honor the Torah. They also use Torah to argue against the Torah and move beyond it — much as a jazz musician orients around a melody, but encircles and departs from and finally returns in service to it. If the central claim of the Torah is God's fidelity, then the prophets point out the gaps between God's promises and the disturbing actualities of the world — and provoke God and the community to attend to them. Reading the prophets forces us to recognize, first, that they were not simply bold rational observers. Rather, Brueggemann states,

> ...they were persons who could be impinged by the spiritual reality that lay outside royal rationality...so one may say the prophets are crazy...or one may say they are free. The prophets of Israel tend to be the voices of "peripheral communities," peripheral in terms of social power, and therefore peripheral in terms of religious perception.... What is offered as the word of the Lord is often not far removed from the passionate agenda of the community.[10]

The prophets evoke the live word of God to attend to the passionate cries and disruptions coming from the periphery of communities. As Abraham Heschel notes, the shatteredness of the prophets reflects God's own shatteredness. The pathos of the prophets participates in God's own pathos.[11]

The "managerial mentality" — which seeks to exploit people to their own advantage — wishes to reduce language to prose, the language of the royal empire, more useful in programs of control. But the prophets refuse this reduction. We can characterize their prophetic word as poetic imagination: the creation of new metaphors for reorienting Israel's imagination. "Hear this word, you cows of Bashan on Mount Samaria, you women who oppress the poor and crush the needy and say to your husbands, 'Bring us some drinks!' " (Amos 4:1). The prophet Amos compares the wanton and oppressive rulers of Israel to those full and wanton beasts that hurt the weaker cattle; in so doing, he is using these strong metaphors to create a new perceptual field through which people can view the abuses of their rulers.

The prophets create an alternative context for humanness by creating a different presumptive world. With new and different images of the world, birthed in poetry, the prophets imagine new and different ways of being human; they envision a world other than that which has become normalized at the hands of oppressors. Prophecy is more than new content; it is a word of passion. Prophecy speaks in new ways, opening the community to new perspectives on God's work among the people.

In contemporary culture, we frequently find the stories of Jesus interpreted in ways that support consumerism, greed, nationalism, and militarism. Some reduce the Christian "salvation" to a spiritual commodity easily consumed by individuals without regard for the world's healing. Such a limited salvation does not confront the greedy ways we form ourselves as a society, and ignores the free God who in Jesus scandalized political and religious systems. Repeatedly in history, the Christian church has allowed its stories and images to be co-opted, while cultural assumptions become the official state religion. These religions blend insidiously into the culture of the church, reducing theological language to harmless ideas and practices that serve the status quo. Such language, in the end, fails to take seriously the abuses that girls like Anna face daily in their schools.

The prophetic vocation of youth

Our dance with God requires more than education in Torah. The foundational stories and practices of the Christian faith — or Torah — under the influence of economic, political, or cultural powers, lend themselves to assimilation to dominant culture. We also require prophetic leadership that points to the gaps between the promises of the Torah and our lived reality. As Craig Dykstra notes, youth in particular need foundational Christian stories to help them engage the contradictions in their world. However, on my reckoning, youth also stand particularly well suited for a prophetic role. Dykstra notes, youth operate within a developmental stage which drives them to seek a coherent hermeneutic or ideology through which to understand the world. But this same search for ideological coherence provides a unique perspective from which they can identify inconsistencies. Not only do young people experience contradictions as logical inconsistencies, but they are particularly touched by the suffering of people and creation. And much like the Old Testament prophets, they find extremely creative ways to express their feelings. As noted by linguists, young people are the most prolific source of new terms and expressions. Additionally, as discovered by the music industry, youth are also a fount of creative expression — however exploited and commercialized. Adults often experience this idealistic passion negatively as "trouble making," but the questioning, challenging, and creativity of young people actually represent a prophetic gift to Christian congregations.

Many congregations make the mistake of relegating young people to a mere passive role of receiving the foundational stories of the Christian faith, while neglecting young people's role of questioning, challenging hypocrisy, seeking justice, and creating beauty. Ignoring such gifts risks encouraging youth to deem the church irrelevant to the suffering world and to their own felt concerns. It is sad to meet bright, passionate young people who have abandoned churches that did not make space for their prophetic gifts of questioning and challenging the status quo.

Today, many young people are finding meaning in seeking justice. They are protesting the injustices of sweatshop labor, exploitation by global capitalism, IMF and World Bank practices that destroy indigenous economies, U.S. involvement in training right-wing dictatorships, and foreign policies that include threats of war. We must ask how the church can make room for such prophetic voices in our midst. We must seek not only to form youth in a static religious culture, but also to include practices that keep us receptive to God's work through young people. Quite simply, through young people, we may find that God is leading us in the dance. As we invite them into the dance with God, they open us to new ways of extending God's truth into places ignored in our stable views and ways. We must encourage young people like Anna Ramirez to feel anger, to ask questions of the church that provoke careful thinking about social and cultural injustices, including the "everyday" objectification of young women's bodies.

The uniqueness of the Christian story

While Brueggemann's and Dykstra's insistence upon the importance of the Torah for the formation of an alternate identity as a hedge against a distorted culture is important, the Christian story is also important because it helps foster a particular identity. For that matter, so do the stories of the Rotarians, Daughters of the American Revolution, or the Aryan Brotherhood. As Brueggemann and Dykstra would agree, the Christianity story involves an incredible story that brings hope to human life. The Christian story, far from establishing mere tribal identity, reveals a subversive grace at play in the midst of the world's brokenness, opening creatures to their true glory and to each other, making the world anew. This story opens us to life in individual and corporate fullness.

Theologian Jürgen Moltmann claims that, although the Bible is filled to the brim with future hope of a messianic kingdom, for too long the church has banished to a distant "beyond" that future hope which is its ground. This hope for a reconciled creation is the "key in which ... everything in it is set, the glow that suffuses everything here in the dawn of an expected new day."[12] We must not imagine Jesus's resurrection as accomplishing merely an otherworldly salvation, but as revealing a future in which the Spirit finally will bring about the completion of this world. Easter thus stands as an act of God's faithfulness; it forms the ground of the promise of the still-outstanding future of Jesus Christ.

Such faith in the faithfulness of God, for us, turns into the expectation of faithfulness and power in history. This expectation of a new world chafes against our experience of this broken world. As Christians, our dealings in history can be understood through eschatological hermeneutics, as "arousing in the past all that has not yet had an opportunity to live as it was meant to."[13] Our dreams reach into our past to our unfulfilled yearnings and project them forward to their fulfillment in God's reign, while calling us to participate with God in the transformation of this present world. Our dreams of fullness opened by grace, draw us ever toward God, neighbor, and true selfhood, and they function as a powerful antidote to the toxic distortions that diminish fullness of life. This is the hope of the gospel, the dream upon which the church is founded, and the story around which we must invite young people to orient themselves.

The practices of remembering and dreaming

One way of ensuring that Christian communities and their youth do not merely embrace a static or domesticated religious tradition is to engage young people in deliberately focusing theological reflection and prayer around specific questions that touch their lives. It is one thing for congregations to grasp doctrines such as Christology, but quite another to extend theological logic to issues that touch the lives of youth and congregations — such as, for example, consumerism, drug abuse, sexuality, exploitation of labor and raw resources, politics, family relationships, entertainment, and involvement with juvenile justice systems. Unless Christian faith has something to say about these and other dimensions of human life, the Christian church risks being domesticated by forces that are not shy about determining them. And worse, once seduced by cultural forces such as consumerism or nationalism, the church sometimes engages in awkward theological gymnastics of justifying or supporting our addictions — to power, acquisition, status, or national or tribal identities — in ways that would not be recognizable to Jesus or the witness of the saints throughout history. The Christian story can be a great gift to young people struggling to find themselves in the midst of a commercial culture that thrives on keeping them in thrall to commodities. But youth also yearn to engage Christian theology in ways relevant to their perceptions of injustice that inhibit the faithfulness of the church. In order to fully engage young people in their prophetic vocation, congregations require practices of discernment, especially remembering and dreaming.

In previous chapters, discernment has been concerned with the heart's expressions of pain or joy, and the mind's search to understand the world in which pain or joy erupts. Yet discernment must also include remembering and keeping dreaming — or seeking God's direction in relation to situations revealed by the heart as places where human life is limited or full. Remembering and dreaming connect our stories — including our deep yearnings for our own and the world's reconciliation. Remembering includes attending through prayer and contemplation to the yearnings of our hearts and those of a broken world. Dreaming includes bringing into view the perspectives of the Christian community, as expressed in scriptures, traditions, writings, practices, and liturgies. Dreaming also involves young people in creating prophetic perspectives that draw from the Christian story, but which also illuminate the gaps and contradictions entailed in a colonized or domesticated church. To help us practice prayer and contemplation with young people and to help us engage young people in the Christian story, let's explore the following ways that youth and adults together might participate in some creative options for cultivating the Christian dream of an alternative world.

Bible study

Youth groups commonly explore the logic of God through disciplined study of the Bible. Many resources exist for studying the Bible with youth groups today. While many curriculum writers develop materials for youth on such topics as sex and dating, parental conflict, peer relationships, violence, and the influence of the media, few focus on police abuse in minority communities, consumerism, women's body image, the difficulties of identity formation in an image culture, or the ways that commodity culture distorts our relationships through competition. Introducing the latter themes necessarily remains a fluid and responsive enterprise; many themes that emerge will be unique or particular to the social location of the church or youth group. For example, one church youth group in California lived in fear of being shot outside of their church building. Their Bible studies focused on fear and courage in the Christian life. Moreover, youth groups need not rely solely on printed curriculum to study the Bible. Youth groups can orient their Bible studies around concrete themes of their lives through the use of concordances and word studies. Youth make some of the most interesting connections when they simply read through the Bible together and ask probing questions. The youth minister, pastor, or youth leaders can help youth read their lives through the odd stories of the Bible, and understand the Bible through the odd stories of their lives. Some connections emerge only after much brooding and struggling together.

Many people interpret biblical materials to fit certain ideological commitments, particularly those that serve to protect the status quo. Walter Brueggemann recommends a humble posture before the scriptural text. That is, we should not consider ourselves to be scripture's masters, forcing it to fit our modes of knowledge and control; we should serve instead as scripture's advocate. In other words, he asserts that the canon of scripture provides the paradigm through which the faithful practice imaginative and creative speech. In fact, this mode of imaginative construal of reality through the materials of the biblical texts is the mode used in the Bible itself, as characters in one location used materials in another for new or redefined purposes. The text thus constitutes the material substance and arena for the practice of imagination. Christian proclamation, as such, is the enterprise of imagining the world through the rhetoric of biblical texts. The Christian act stands as a construal of reality, displacing the dominant social reality that has been accepted and habituated.

In telling our stories to each other against the backdrop of the raw and imagistic material of the Bible, we begin to talk and imagine our way into a faithful future. Brueggemann suggests the guiding metaphor of a therapist who helps patients surface old memories one by one. Over time as forgotten memories surface, the patient, in conversation with the therapist, constructs an alternative story of his or her life. In Brueggemann's view, imagining alternatives is not the work of some remote theologian, but is rightfully the work of the community, even the young. Much as the therapist helps raise forgotten memories, the role of pastoral leadership entails placing before the congregation the raw biblical stories as images, ideas, and perspectives. We are to resist overanalyzing the texts; too much of historical criticism has written some troublesome images out of the text. For patients in therapy, Brueggemann says, oftentimes precisely the most troublesome memories eventually reveal themselves to us as a source of transformation. Similarly, troublesome biblical texts often contain ideas and images that help put the world together in new ways.

Many times we fail to find a place for troublesome memories or texts because we have become engrained in habits of life that do not allow us to consider alternatives. Together, however, the texts of scripture and our lives present multiple opportunities to challenge these established patterns. As we brood over biblical ideas and images, we struggle with others to make sense of them by talking our way into some new orientation or perspective. Making space for forgotten texts of the Bible, in turn, might also bring to the surface forgotten dimensions of our own lives whose details require careful contemplation. In short, openness to the biblical text and its transformative power remains both essential for the questioning and creativity of youth. Such openness invites youth not to a passive role, but to an imaginative role of interpreting the Bible in view of their lives, and interpreting their lives in view of the Bible. Bibliodrama and Lectio Divina especially are two ways to engage youth in Bible study.

Bibliodrama

Drama offers an important resource for facilitating this process of brooding over the scriptures. Bibliodrama is a kind of midrash, or an ancient form of reading between the lines of the scripture stories that aims to seek deeper and self-implicating meanings. For the rabbis, midrash or interpretive engagement with the Bible often manifested itself in wordplays, analogies, and even puns, which intensified the active experience of reading texts. "Midrash" is derived from the Hebrew root that means to investigate or explore. In the midrash readers closely examine the written text for meanings and insights that enrich understanding and enhance one's relationship to the Bible.

Bibliodrama is a form of role-playing in which the roles played are taken from biblical texts. The roles may be those of characters who appear in the Bible, either explicitly and by name (Adam or Eve) or implicitly, that is, persons whose presence may be inferred from an imaginative reading of the stories (Noah's wife or Abraham's mother). In Bibliodrama, the available roles or parts can even include certain objects or images capable of being acted out in voice and action (the serpent in the Garden or the staff of Moses). Places can speak (the Jordan River or Mount Sinai). Spiritual figures can also talk (angels, or God, or the Adversary). Then there appears a host of characters from the legendary tradition (Lilith or the five perverted judges of Sodom) who can similarly be invited onto the bibliodramatic stage. Below is a brief example that illustrates how a session of Bibliodrama might look when conducted with youth.[14]

A class is in progress: a group of fifteen youth are seated in a circle, studying the Bible. We have been reading the story of the Garden of Eden and have come to the end of that story, arriving at the lines that say: "Therefore the Lord God sent him forth from the Garden of Eden to till the ground whence he was taken. So he drove out the man" (Gen. 3:23–24).

Rather than talking about this episode and giving our ideas about it, I propose to the class that we step into it and play it out. "Let's look at this scene in a bibliodramatic way," I suggest. "Let's see what Eve has to say about this moment of expulsion." The class, familiar with this approach from previous experiences, accepts this suggestion with nods of assent. "So, I'd like you to imagine that you *are Eve* at this moment in the story. Tell us, Eve, what is this like for you?"

Hands go up, each hand a potential voice of Eve.

"I am furious at the deception God practiced on us, the temptation, the duplicity, the curse. It will take me a long time, if ever, before I trust God again."

"Driven out is right. I don't want to leave. I straggle. I hide. I look back. All I know is being left behind."

"You know, it says in the story that God 'drove the man out,' but nothing is said of me. Here is another place where I feel invisible. This whole thing is always between God and Adam."

"But that's the point," says another participant. "You see, I am not being driven out. It's Adam who is all nostalgic and depressed. I can't wait to get out of here, anymore than I could wait to eat the apple. Eden is a place where I have no part to play, no future. It *has* all been Adam and God. In this world we're going to, there's going to be lots for me to do."

"So you feel...?" I ask.

"I have a sense of power and possibility. There's something coming. I have a purpose. I am to be 'the mother of all living.' Now that's a part to play."

"Not a bad exchange, if you ask me," someone adds by way of comment.

Another hand is raised, a man speaks as Eve: "It's even more than that. In a certain way, I don't really leave Eden at all, ever. Only Adam leaves. He really is banished. He's never going to know again what it feels like to be part of life in the way he is here. He goes into exile. But a part of me stays here. A part of me can go back. The garden is the womb, and I have that inside me."

"Can I speak for Adam?" another participant asks.

"Sure."

"I do feel the curse falling directly on me. Eve is not included in this expulsion. And yet she does come with me. Why?"

"I choose to go."

"Yes, but why?"

"I choose because it is what I want. I want out and I want a life with you. We were created *together.* Whichever way you want to think about how we came to be, it is clear that we belong together."

"I was angry at you because you caused us to lose the Garden."

"Well, I was angry at you that there was no place in that Garden for me, even for us. It was all you and God."

"So you deliberately..."

"Well, we have to give the serpent some credit."

"Where is that serpent anyway?"

"Here I am," says one of the group members, playfully easing himself from his chair to the floor.

"Are you coming with us?" Eve asks.

"He'll be nothing but trouble," says Adam. "You heard what God said about 'enmity' and 'bruising.'"

"Well," says the serpent, "you heard what God said about eating and dying. And here you are."

"I don't understand," says Adam, looking genuinely bewildered, "you're not saying that God is not to be trusted...are you?"

"Let's just say that with God you cannot always trust your human sense of things. Nothing is ever quite the way it seems."

"Let's take him with us," says Eve. "I think we're going to need him."

Lectio Divina — "Holy Reading"[15]

The Latin phrase *lectio divina*, difficult to translate into English, literally means "divine reading" or "sacred reading." *Lectio divina* ordinarily involves a slow perusal of sacred scripture, both the Old and New Testaments. It is not undertaken with the intention of gaining information but of using the texts as an aid to contact the living God. While it is most commonly used to meditate on a passage of scripture, it is also used as an approach to listening for the voice of God amid particular circumstances, events, or situations. In this case, the "text" becomes the memory of our experiences. I have sometimes used this approach as a means of inviting young people to remember the experiences and situations explored in the course of their discernment — in the movements of listening and understanding — with a view to hearing God's voice.

Preparation. Consider forming groups of no more than eight. For each group, ask three persons to prepare to read the *lectio* text (any biblical passage chosen to reflect upon) — one for each of the three times the text is read. Include readers of both genders. Find a chime or bell that can be used to signal the end of silent meditation periods.

Get a candle and matches. If you wish, choose a song for the group to sing together before beginning. You may find a song that the group likes to sing every time they begin *lectio divina*.

Opening. When the group has gathered, describe the process for this time of meditation on scripture. Explain that the same passage of scripture will be read three times.

A time of silence will follow each reading. The bell will end the silence and introduce a time to share. Explain that you will instruct them on what they are to listen for before each reading of the passage. Explain now that during the first reading, they will hear the passage twice. They should listen for a word that stands out for them, that seems to "shine" or "shimmer." When everyone is seated comfortably, say, "We make our beginning in the name of Christ, in the light of the Living Word." Light the candle, explaining that this act reminds us of Christ's presence in our midst. Help the group members to become quiet and fully aware of God's presence by taking a few moments to relax and to say a silent prayer welcoming God into this time.

First reading. The first reader reads the passage aloud two times, pausing for a moment after the first reading. The hearers listen for the word God speaks to them from this passage while it is being read. When the text has been read twice, allow two to three minutes of silence. Then ring the bell. Ask persons to share just the word or phrase God has given to them with no other explanation or comment. You may choose to go around the circle and have each person share, or ask persons to share when or if they feel comfortable. After this sharing, instruct participants to listen to the next reading and to ponder how the passage seems to touch their lives. Ask them to listen for the answer to this question: "How is my life touched by this passage?"

Second reading. The second reader reads the passage one time. Following the reading, wait a few minutes, then ring the bell. Ask persons to share in one sentence how what they have heard has touched them. After this sharing, instruct group members to listen to the passage one more time, asking themselves, "Is there an invitation here? Do I sense that this passage is inviting me to do or be something?"

Third reading. The third reader reads the passage one last time. Following the reading, allow a few minutes of meditation time as each person tries to hear what Christ wants him or her to be or do today in response to the reading. The answer might be a contemplative one, a better way of being in God's presence, or it might be an action to be carried out. After you ring the bell, ask persons to share what they have heard from God.

Closing. Conclude with "Go Now in Peace" or a song or blessing that affirms the ever-present love of Christ.

Forum theater

Forum theater, developed in Brazil by Augusto Boal, provides a useful tool for communal discernment and is now widely used by activists the world over. Religious groups around the globe have also used Boal's work for helping religious communities bring their faith into conversation with the world. This theater game can be described in its barest form as follows.[16]

1. A group discusses some common tension that exists within their community contexts. Together they develop a brief play that articulates a problem. This skit must clearly include an antagonist and a protagonist with different ideologies representing the real-life situations discussed earlier.

2. The actors act out the "problem" up to the point of its peak of conflict, but without any resolution of the problem. The conclusions offered by actors should represent the typical ways such problems are played out in the community.

3. The spect-actors (the Boalian term for those who are not involved in the original play but are later drawn into it) are asked if they agree with the solutions advanced by the protagonist. They are then told that the play is going to be done a second time. This time, as the actors try to present the same play with the same problems, the spectators stop the action by yelling "freeze." One at a time the audience members jump into the scene to take the protagonist's place with a new solution to the problem. The aim

is not to represent the world as it is, but to show it as it could be if different solutions were offered.

4. The scene may be acted dozens of times, with the spect-actors attempting various solutions to the problem. At some point, as the group identifies different solutions to the problem, the director may find it helpful to give new instructions, such as "Play the role as Jesus might." These instructions may spark a new round of ideas about solutions to the problem.

5. After each round of new responses, the director should debrief each new character: "What were you trying to accomplish? What were your methods?" To the original players, the director might direct questions such as, "How did this solution feel for you?" "Do you think this solution would work better? Why? Why not?"

6. At some point the players may find themselves breaking out of their original roles, swayed by the actions of the spect-actors and their new responses.

7. The forum is over when the group feels it has identified new, more faithful strategies for engaging the problems of their community.

Image theater

Another theater game that can be used to engage young people in rethinking the odd stories of our lives in light of God's Word, stems from a repertoire of skills known as image theater. Instead of creating skits or vignettes, this form of drama utilizes frozen forms or images formed by many people around some theme of their lives. One I have used with much success is called "machine of images." I outlined the idea of the "machine" in chapter 4, but here I want to share how I use this process to explore the topic of "the church."

In order to warm up, to get people out of their heads, I invite groups to form a circle and, one at a time, to step into the center of the circle and arrange their bodies as a small piece of a machine, using rhythmic movement and sound (no words). Each person steps into the center and connects his or her body in some relationship with the machine that the other youth have already started constructing.

When completed, the machine includes all members of the circle in a connected mass of rhythm and sound. But this is only the warm-up for the next game, in which I assign to the machine a theme such as "the church." One by one, youth move to the center of the circle and arrange themselves into some image that depicts a dimension of their experience of the church, again using sound and movement. Among the common depictions are the glories of worship, the authoritarian leadership of the pastor, the church reaching out to the homeless, and the church ignoring its own youth. In the end, the machine constitutes a complex moving sculpture of the church.

Debriefing the machine game can take place in various ways. I usually begin by asking participants to say what they think the machine means, and very interesting interpretations often emerge. Only after everyone has had a chance to add his or her interpretation of the machine's parts do I invite members of the machine to state their own intentions. Usually, this conversation opens into a complex discussion of the blessings and problems of the church. When the conversation has accomplished its purpose — that is, when it has opened us to the blessings and problems of the church — once again I ask the members to take their places in the machine and freeze. Then I ask those participants who have not taken a place in the machine (if any remain) to speak quietly a word from the Bible to the machine. How would God speak to the church as depicted by this machine? The members call to mind some word from scripture that comforts or challenges the church. I might also close in prayer, asking participants to identify some way they feel God speaking to them.

Study of saints

Youth can also be opened to new perspectives about the logic of God through studying, acting out, or watching movies about the lives of saints. When young people see the ways Christians throughout history have responded to their love of God and neighbor, they too can be inspired and provoked to new understandings of their own possibilities. Too often, our images of the Christian life become stiff and rigid. Presenting stories of real people and their lives, however, makes the Christian faith come alive. The story of St. Francis, to take just one example, evokes questions about how we relate to material things within a life of faith. Similarly, the story of Mother Teresa evokes questions about how we value (or fail to value) other people.

Way-of-life practices

At certain times, particularly during crises, the Christian faith often enjoys a fairly direct influence on our lives. For the most part, however, many of us feel everyday pressures distorting our relationship with God, and more specifically, impinging on our relations to each other, the earth, and to strangers. The forces of commodity culture seem so powerful that the Christian faith often appears limited to a mere affiliation or stated identity. Such a faith remains insufficient for loving God and neighbor and for participating fully in God's reign of peace and justice. If we want once again to cultivate human virtues of love, trust, community, generosity, mutual appreciation, respect, and gratitude, we must deliberately seek habits of life that foster these virtues. If we are to engage fully the dance of grace, we must seek appropriate ways to respond to the music of God's love that we hear. Christians throughout history have discovered steps to this dance or practices that foster partnership with God. Christian practices — the concrete ways we shape the activities of our lives — have defined Christian faithfulness and the possibility of deeper truth about God, world, and self.

Christian practices are concrete ways of inviting God's presence among us and of seeking partnership with God's work in the world. They open us to new awareness and help us dream for and with the world. Consider a few suggestions for Christian practices to try out with youth.

1. Worshiping God together: praising God, giving thanks for God's creative and redemptive work in the world, hearing God's Word preached, and receiving the sacraments given to us in Christ.

2. Telling the Christian story to one another: reading and hearing the scriptures and the stories of the church's experience through history.

3. Interpreting together the scriptures and the history of the church's experience, particularly in relation to their meaning for our own lives in the world.

4. Praying together and by ourselves, not only in formal services of worship but in all times and places.

5. Confessing our sins to one another, forgiving and becoming reconciled with one another.

6. Tolerating one another's failures and encouraging one another in the work each must do and the vocation each must live.

7. Carrying out specific faithful acts of service and witness together.

8. Giving generously of one's means and receiving gratefully gifts others have to give.

9. Suffering with and for one another and all whom Jesus showed us to be our neighbors.

10. Providing hospitality and care, not only to one another but to strangers and even enemies.

11. Listening and talking attentively to one another about our particular experiences in life.

12. Struggling together to become conscious of and to understand the nature of the context in which we live.

13. Criticizing and resisting all those powers and patterns (both within the church and in the world as a whole) that destroy human beings, corrode human community, and injure God's creation.

14. Working together to maintain and create social structures and institutions that sustain life in the world in ways that accord with God's will.[17]

While the preceding list is not complete, it includes key suggestions about Christian ways of being in the world. A full elaboration of the importance of Christian practices is beyond the scope of this book, but a few key reminders about the benefits of practices may help you in your ministry.

- Practices connect our stories to the story of God.

- Practices are ways of concretely responding to what we know about God's work in the world.

- Practices are best done alongside a community of people who seek to support each other in this lifestyle.

- Practices are ways people seek to embody their commitments to God — with their entire selves, heart, mind, soul, and body.

- Practices involve an exploration of excellence, as we seek to improve our skills for the practice undertaken.

- Practices engage us in activities, relationships, and thoughts that open us to new understandings of God, neighbor, and self.

- Practicing our faith in the context of an ecology of lifestyle practices does not lead to a static view of God, neighbor, and self, but opens us to the living Word of God, that leads us ever on in humility and strength — from faith to faith.

These practices help connect our lives to the grace that surrounds us and to others whose lives are woven into the same web of grace. In the context of these relationships and practices, our dreams look very different than when we unreflectively assimilate ourselves into our culture. Living into these practices means ordering our lives in ways that run counter to many of those sponsored by our culture. These new relationships can make some theological truths more concrete or evident, and bear directly on the issues and circumstances that trouble youth.

Interviews with a pastor

Youth need the wealth of experience that can be drawn from older people who have sought to be faithful throughout their lives. If young people are seeking God's logic in relation to some particular concern, they may find it helpful to have an hour or two to explore particular issues with their pastor. Pastors with years of exegetical experience and a familiarity with texts and theological ideas can be a great resource for the searching faith of young people. Such conversations also provide an opportunity for pastors to connect with the lives and questions of youth. Yet the conversation need not be one-sided. Young people can bring fresh perspectives on biblical texts and themes that enrich pastors' minds and hearts as well.

Songs

Songs and hymns of the Christian tradition offer another resource for theological ideas. Reading through the words of hymns can prompt interesting questions, including concerns about such ancient terms as ebenezer, sanctification, and redeemer. Exploring such questions might also open youth to the history of their faith tradition, connecting their lives to a people whose history extends back thousands of years. Hymns and songs also contain ideas with contemporary application. Youth may be surprised to find that their ancestors explored many of their own twenty-first-century questions. Often youth feel their lives to be unlike anything that has gone before them. But exploring hymns and songs may reveal ways our ancestors have faced similar questions and grappled with issues of idolatry, consumerism, violence, or distraction from love of God and neighbor. Adults who help young people make such historic connections provide them with a crucial resource and connect them to a visionary movement larger than that offered by their own peer group.

Creating and singing songs is not simply an intellectual exercise, but involves the heart and soul. Indeed, much of Christian scripture emerges from such evocative expression. Songs often draw from scripture, but also create new metaphors to describe God's work in our midst. Much as Brueggemann describes the prophetic imagination, songs can create a new lens through which can be described the world and God's work in it. Creating songs is an important way of keeping Christian faith fresh, but also of resisting the dominant stories of culture that seek to dull and deaden our lives. Young people may turn to the songs of our heritage as a rich source of wisdom, especially when seeking more redemptive ways of seeing the world's wounds and blessings, and when seeking faithful ways of seeing the particular issues that touch their lives.

Church statements

Exploring themes introduced by youth provides an opportunity for adults to introduce their young people to general statements made by the larger church. Catholic churches and many mainline Protestant churches have social principles, papal encyclicals, or statements issued by churchwide boards or agencies representing a larger theological tradition. Many of these statements have direct or indirect relevance to themes or analyses that young people explore. I would add here that many adults are similarly unfamiliar with such statements — so studying them often educates the parents as much as informing our youth!

One story of remembering and dreaming

In previous chapters, we observed how one group of young people explored the following theme and situation: "Some African American males are angry because of unfair treatment in the juvenile justice system." When they *listened* to their hearts — through conversation, timed writing, prayer, drama, and art — they discovered a common tension that they lived with in their community. When they engaged this theme, analyzing it with their minds — through empirical studies, conversations with experts, reading, Internet research, and dramatic representations — they gained a degree of *understanding* about the causes for the theme and its situations. This is the story of what they did when they turned to the soul portion of their discernment: the remembering and dreaming.

In order to remind themselves of the situations they were engaging — the situations that made them angry, sad, and frustrated — they posted on the wall of their classroom pictures and drawings of the various situations that surfaced in their original conversations, including young black boys being stopped by police, shopkeepers expecting shoplifting hovering over black youth, black boys and men in prison. Beside those pictures, the group posted a large chart representing relationships and connections they discovered that explained some of the reasons for black boys' involvement in the justice system. These relationships and connections ranged from local and national political decisions and public policies to media portrayal of black men as violent, the disenfranchisement of black communities from the political process, unemployment in some communities, illegal redlining of urban communities by banks, and racist attitudes among some law enforcement authorities. Then the young people drew lines and arrows indicating relationships between the influences. For example, they drew a line between media portrayals of black boys as violent and racist attitudes among police and an arrow between that and black boys being stopped more frequently by police. Of course, this is only one stream of influence. No one situation can be explained by one stream alone. Most situations involve multiple causes. Their charts depicted the causes more as a web than a stream flowing in one direction.

In *remembering* and *dreaming,* this group of young people sought to orient their theme and its causes in the context of God's work in the world. The question that guided their reflection was, "What does God think or feel about this situation?" More specifically, what does God think or feel about African American males' unfair treatment in the juvenile justice system, political decisions and public policies, media portrayal of black men as violent, the disenfranchisement of black communities from the political process, unemployment in some communities, illegal redlining of urban communities by banks, and racist attitudes among some law enforcement authorities? Below are some of the ways this group decided to explore these issues.

Bible studies

A small group from the group of twelve explored the topic of racism in the Bible. Specifically, they offered several key passages as examples of Jesus's feelings about ethnicity. One example involves God's revelation to Peter concerning God's mission among all people.

The next day Peter started out with them, and some of the brothers from Joppa went along. The following day he arrived in Caesarea. Cornelius was expecting them and had called together his relatives and close friends. As Peter entered the house, Cornelius met him and fell at his feet in reverence. But Peter made him get up. "Stand up," he said, "I am only a man myself."

Talking with him, Peter went inside and found a large gathering of people. He said to them: "You are well aware that it is against our law for a Jew to associate with a Gentile or visit him. But God has shown me that I should not call any man impure or unclean. So when I was sent for, I came without raising any objection. May I ask why you sent for me?"

Cornelius answered: "Four days ago I was in my house praying at this hour, at three in the afternoon. Suddenly a man in shining clothes stood before me and said, 'Cornelius, God has heard your prayer and remembered your gifts to the poor. Send to Joppa for Simon who is called Peter. He is a guest in the home of Simon the tanner, who lives by the sea.' So I sent for you immediately, and it was good of you to come. Now we are all here in the presence of God to listen to everything the Lord has commanded you to tell us."

Then Peter began to speak: "I now realize how true it is that God does not show favoritism but accepts men from every nation who fear him and do what is right." (Acts 10:24–35)

The group drew conclusions from this passage, including God's love of all ethnic groups.

Conversation with a pastor

The group invited a local pastor to join them in a question-and-answer session about racism. This pastor had a role in the civil rights movement of the 1960s and shared with the group some of this history, as well as some of the theological ideas of liberation, rooted in images of the exodus of the Israelites from Egypt. Other topics explored in this conversation included how to think about media exploitation of black youth, and the marginalization of black communities in the political process.

Exploring church statements

Many young people in this group attended mainline Protestant churches that have generated specific statements about such issues as racism, commercial exploitation, and community political processes. For example, the United Methodist Church has in its Social Principles the following statement on racism:

> *Racism* is the combination of the power to dominate by one race over other races and a value system that assumes that the dominant race is innately superior to the others. Racism includes both personal and institutional racism. Personal racism is manifested through the individual expressions, attitudes, and/or behaviors that accept the assumptions of a racist value system and that maintain the benefits of this system. Institutional racism is the established social pattern that supports implicitly or explicitly the racist value system. Racism plagues and cripples our growth in Christ, inasmuch as it is antithetical to the gospel itself. White people are unfairly granted privileges and benefits that are denied to persons of color. Therefore, we recognize racism as sin and affirm the ultimate and temporal worth of all persons. We rejoice in the gifts that particular ethnic histories and cultures bring to our total life. We commend and encourage the self-awareness of all racial and ethnic groups and oppressed people that leads them to demand their just and equal rights as members of society. We assert the obligation of society and groups within the society to implement compensatory programs that redress long-standing, systemic social deprivation of racial and ethnic people. We further assert the right of members of racial and ethnic groups to equal opportunities in employment and promotion; to education and training of the highest quality; to nondiscrimination in voting, in access to public accommodations, and in housing purchase or rental; to credit, financial

loans, venture capital, and insurance policies; and to positions
of leadership and power in all elements of our life together. We
support affirmative action as one method of addressing the in-
equalities and discriminatory practices within our church and
society.[18]

Exploring these statements in light of their particular issue helped
them to know that the church deems it important to speak to issues
that touch even them. These statements also helped them to know
some ways in which the logic of God can be extended to their particular concerns. Through these documents these young people began
to glimpse God's sadness concerning their particular issue.

Exploring major doctrines

The adult leader of this group introduced the group to doctrines of the
Creation, Trinity, and the reign of God, and the importance of unity
and diversity in Christian faith. One conclusion from this study was
that all of God's creation — including ethnic groups — is marked by
God's beauty, love, and creativity, and contains the yearning for and
possibility of communion with God and neighbor. The study of the
Trinity and the reign of God revealed God's design that all creatures
join in unity, as in the Trinity, but not in such a way that obliterates
our particularity, but rather in a manner that enhances our unique
gifts for the community of God.

Image theater

As a final activity, this group was asked to position themselves into a
living sculpture that expressed their findings about the theme and its
causes. One by one the young people took their place in a tableau that
represented the original theme — a young black boy being stopped by
police and being taken to jail. Around this frozen image, other youth
took places that represented the various causes of this situation. One
small group froze in the image of a group of rich media corporation
executives who were like puppet masters controlling one black boy
holding a gun. Others created a small group of empowered officials

who were standing tall on chairs with arms folded, surveying the room — yet they were ignoring the young people getting arrested. When the image was completed, the young people were asked to look around them without removing themselves from the image.

As the group finished their image, the group was asked to take a seat on the floor with eyes closed. The adult facilitator led the group in a guided meditation in which they were asked to picture in their minds the image they had created. As they had the picture firm in their imaginations, they were asked to picture Jesus entering the room. They were asked to imagine what Jesus might say to each of the figures in the sculpture. When the group had sufficient time, they were asked to once again return to their place in the sculpture. They were told to form themselves, in silence, into an image that they think would please Jesus. The group spent a few minutes and gradually took their places in a sculpture that depicted more just and loving relationships among all involved.

The above activities engaged a group of twelve youth and one adult in discerning God's heart and mind in relation to one theme from their lives. This report is not a complete account but suggests the range of activities that one group conducted.

The intrinsic goodness of remembering and dreaming

It is important to view the practices of this third movement, remembering and dreaming, as valuable in the process of discernment, but also as valuable in their own right. Healing occurs when young people connect their lives to the life of God. Young people have little space in their lives for silence and solitude. As they make deliberate space for prayer and contemplation, they often find a new kind of center to their lives — a center focused on greater awareness of God, neighbor, and themselves. The habit of prayer and contemplation opens for them the possibility of seeing all other people and creation as they truly are — their wounds and their gifts. This new perspective creates greater compassion for others and self.

Healing also occurs when young people learn to see their lives and worlds from the perspective of God's work in the world. The commercial culture of youth is largely devoid of any sense of history, hence many youth live with a sense of loneliness and isolation in the cosmos. As young people engage in theological reflection, they come to see their lives as part of a great history, minimizing their sense of loneliness. Christian faith — its ideas and embodied practices — provides a sense of identity that is crucial for young people. Such identity can help give meaning to their diverse experiences in the postmodern world.

Christian youth ministry that introduces Christian faith only as an abstract set of ideas is a problem. Young people are particularly disturbed by ideas that have no direct relationship with their lives or the world. I am sometimes asked about the relationship of discernment to evangelism. I do not want to claim too much, but there are examples of young people for whom Christian faith has meant little until their exploration of particular themes brought the gospel into relationship with their concrete lives. Some young people already feel deep concern for the wounds of the world, but they do not see Christian faith as relevant to these wounds. When they discover that Christian faith is deeply involved in the reconciliation of this world, they have an increased appreciation for Christian faith. Many young people who are not especially attracted by the ideas and doctrines of Christian faith are moved by the beauty of a community of youth and adults *embodying* faith in Christ.

Notes

1. Some have inquired about the distinctions between *remembering* and *listening*. There is a structural similarity between the two movements, because they both rely upon intuition or affect, and the ways of practicing them often overlap — for example, using prayer and silence. The *listening* movement can be understood as attuning to significations of tensions and antipathies that exist in the culture, felt in the human heart or body. The *remembering* movement can be thought of as a means of evaluating situations once they have been analyzed critically and theologically. In reality, there is a deep connection between the two movements since it seems likely that those who spend time in prayer focused on concrete life situations may also be

more intuitively attuned to tensions and antipathies in their own hearts and that surface in the world around them. However, the same can be said of work of the mind and body. Their use may make people more attentive to tensions and contradictions, more discerning.

2. Tom Beaudoin, *Virtual Faith: The Irreverent Quest of Generation X* (San Francisco: Jossey-Bass, 2000), 73ff.

3. Stephen D. Jones, *Faith Shaping: Youth and the Experience of Faith* (Valley Forge, Pa.: Judson Press, 1987), 13–22.

4. Walter Brueggemann, *Creative Word: Canon as a Model for Biblical Education* (Minneapolis: Fortress Press, 1982), 13.

5. Ibid., 16.

6. Ibid., 17.

7. Craig Dykstra, *Growing in the Life of Faith: Education and Christian Practices* (Louisville: Geneva Press, 1999), 113.

8. Ibid., 121.

9. Brueggemann, *Creative Word,* 50.

10. Ibid.

11. Cited in ibid., 65.

12. Jürgen Moltmann, *The Spirit of Life: A Universal Affirmation* (Minneapolis: Fortress Press, 2003), 44.

13. Ibid., 54.

14. The information for this section is quoted from *The Reconstructionist: A Journal of Contemporary Jewish Thought.* See Web site www.rrc.edu/journal/recon62_1/bibliodrama.htm. See also Peter Pitzele, *Our Fathers' Wells: A Personal Encounter with the Myths of Genesis* (San Francisco: HarperSanFrancisco, 1995); *Scripture Windows: The Practice of Bibliodrama* (Los Angeles: Alef Design Group, 1998).

15. From Dorothy Bass and Don C. Richter, *Way to Live: Christian Practices for Teens,* Leader's Guide (Nashville: Upper Room Books, 2002), 7. Used with permission of Upper Room Books.

16. Augusto Boal, *Theatre of the Oppressed* (New York: Theatre Communications Group, 1985), and *Games for Actors and Non-Actors* (London and New York: Routledge, 1992).

17. Dykstra, *Growing in the Life of Faith,* 43.

18. From *The Book of Discipline of the United Methodist Church — 2000,* par. 162A (Nashville: United Methodist Publishing House, 2000).

Seven

Acting

Loving God with your strength —
Movement four

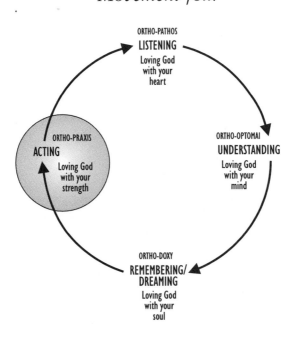

ORTHO-PATHOS
LISTENING
Loving God
with your
heart

ORTHO-OPTOMAI
UNDERSTANDING
Loving God
with your
mind

ORTHO-PRAXIS
ACTING
Loving God
with your
strength

ORTHO-DOXY
**REMEMBERING/
DREAMING**
Loving God
with your
soul

"Right foot blue" are three words Tommy Greer, youth minister of First United Methodist Church, never thought he would hear himself utter. Though he had often chided fellow youth ministers for their gratuitous use of entertainment, he found himself desperate to keep the interest of the approximately sixty bored youth before him. "Left hand yellow," he bellowed, hoping his feigned enthusiasm would spark some response from the teens in attendance. Finally, the six "twisted" bodies brave enough to risk humiliation before their peers succumbed to the laws of physics and tumbled in a heap on the floor, eliciting a few chuckles on behalf of the spectators. As the clock on the back wall of the youth room struck 9:00 p.m. teens rushed toward the door to the parking lot. "That concludes our Bible study on *The Secure Foundation in Christ....* Don't forget the lock-in/movie night next week!" shouted Tommy, as the teens filed out of the church gym to join parents and friends in waiting cars.

As youth departed from the parking lot toward their homes, Tommy Greer retreated to his office and slumped behind his desk piled high with books with titles such as *"100 Youth Group Games, Having Fun with Your Youth Group,* and *Strategies for Lock-ins, Retreats and Parties.* The broken spines of the books are testimony to his desperate attempt to attract youth — to get them here! As he centered himself once again, he took a deep breath and his mind filled with images of the day spent in preparation and the evening spent trying to entertain youth with the church's dwindling resources of volunteers and money. As he turned off the light in his office, Tommy could not prevent the inevitable questions, "What have I offered them tonight worth leaving their homes and friends — or mine for that matter? Am I called by God for more than this?"

Meanwhile, in the church parking lot, fifteen-year-old Janie turned to her friend Melissa and asked, "Are you coming back to youth group next week?" "I don't know, it depends on what else is going on," Melissa replied. As the girls hopped into the back seat of her mom's car, Janie's mother asked, "Was youth group fun tonight? What did you do?" After a brief hesitation Janie exclaimed, "Nothing ... we never do anything!"

Recall the ancient fairy tale "Sleeping Beauty" or "Briar Rose" told by the Brothers Grimm of a beautiful young princess who was cursed by a wicked witch and put under a spell. According to the myth, the spell predicted that the beautiful princess would be pricked by a spindle and sleep for a hundred years. In the older versions of the story, not only did the princess fall fast asleep but so did those around her. Wanderers who occasionally came upon her and her sleeping friends in her forest cottage were said to assume they were dead, except for the red hue in their cheeks. According to the Grimm Brothers' version of this ancient tale, the sleeping princess was awakened by a kiss from a prince.

This tale is not only good bedtime reading for children, but it points to a fear basic to human existence: the fear of being alive but unable to act upon the world, of sleeping through life. This fear takes many forms in fairy tales, myths, horror legends, and religious texts. Myths of zombies, the walking dead, and monsters half alive lurk in the recesses of our minds and represent a profound fear of lost human vitality, of an inability to realize our potential for meaningful activity. In addition to speaking of fear, these tales also speak of a deep human yearning to be fully awakened to life — by a kiss, if possible. As Christians, we proclaim that the gospel of Jesus holds power because it involves a kiss, awakening the possibility of being fully alive. This is the hope of Christian faith in general and youth ministry in particular: to awaken young people to life.

Contemporary adolescence, like the prick of the spindle in the fairy tale, renders young people "asleep" — except for the red hue in their cheeks. This slumber of contemporary adolescence does not involve lack of activity, for indeed their frenetic activity is a sign, like the hue of their cheeks, of their potential. But the slumber of youth involves a lack of meaningful activity in the world. As youth ministers, we are often inspired by the energy and beauty of youth, but saddened by our inability to awaken them to full and meaningful agency as makers of history, as disciples of Jesus turning the world upside down. And we, like Tommy Greer, are haunted by the question of whether contemporary youth ministry represents the sleep-inducing prick of the spindle or an awakening kiss. This is a question we must answer honestly for the sake of our teens and the gospel. Exploring this question requires that we examine the culture of youth and the cultural contexts in which youth are held, including commercial media, education, and church youth groups.

Much of the contemporary slumber, passivity, or domestication of youth is a consequence of the commercial culture that surrounds them. Many youth groups across the United States reenact Tommy

Greer's struggle to attract youth to the church long enough to introduce them to the gospel of Jesus, amid the overwhelming power of
an entertainment industry that teaches young people to expect that
anything of value should be entertaining. While there is nothing intrinsically wrong with entertainment, like many good things it can
become addictive, distracting youth from sources of deeper satisfaction — learning, praying, loving, and working — that awaken them
to full vitality. Popular forms of entertainment promoted by marketers and consumed by young people rarely engage them as active
and creative agents — creating, for example, music, poetry, theater,
relationships, or political justice — but instead encourage them to
passively consume cultural products created elsewhere.

Understanding how youth ministry should relate to entertainment
and cultural products is a key question for the future of youth
ministry, especially if we are to awaken young people to their full
potential. First, culture is not simply an evil to be avoided, but is an
unavoidable context of human social life that is capable of either enhancing or distorting our sensibilities, behaviors, and relationships.
Indeed, there is no such thing as a Christian gospel pure and unpol-
luted by culture. The gospel is intricately wrapped in the ideas and
metaphors of the culture in which Jesus lived, and in order to be fully
intelligible by us must be told in ways that make sense in our culture.
However, Jesus did not merely baptize and adopt the ideas and practices of his culture. While Jesus used the metaphors and ideas from
the culture at hand, he also used them in ways that critiqued cultural habits contemporary to his era such as the exclusion of lepers,
women, and Samaritans.

Today, our struggle is to articulate the gospel in ways familiar to
people living in contemporary American commercial culture, yet we
must be careful to present the gospel in ways that do not obscure
the gospel or its critique of culture. A particular danger of our commercial technological culture is that the cultural media we use to
present the gospel and attract youth — music, videos, high-energy
talks, multimedia, sound-bite technology, and spectacular events —
are not value-neutral, but contain tacit messages about how to act,

think, and feel. Embedded in the media of our technological commercial culture are messages that anything of value can be bought at the cash register, must be sensational, can be done alone, must be very simple to understand, requires little effort on our behalf, involves immediate gratification, and obscures a history that began before or extends beyond me in space and time. Values promoted by popular entertainment and its technological delivery systems contradict much of what Christians have long valued — community, creativity, silence, contemplation, seeking justice, compassion, generosity, and connecting our stories to the story of God.

Not only does the entertainment culture lull youth into a slumber of passive consumption, but many ordinary contexts of adolescent life also collude in this pacification by failing to engage the full capabilities of youth and encouraging their passive consumption. Employment in the service sector, ingesting education while awaiting a promised future of employment, and too often, attending our church youth programs all fulfill someone else's desires for young people and do not engage them as agents in actively shaping history.

The systematic removal of youth from active roles in public life is a feature of modern adolescence. Historians reveal that the contemporary domestication of adolescents in which their movement in the public realm is limited is not grounded in biology or psychology of youth but is socially constructed.

Yet, despite the early history of America in which youth held significant social roles, by the mid-nineteenth century the Industrial Revolution fundamentally changed the nature of work in America. Industrial factory work focused the attention of workers on wages and distracted them from the common good of the community, from creativity and the intrinsic value of work. The conditions of industrial factory work were vastly more dangerous, competitive, and exploitative of people and the environment. While it made sense for young people to work alongside their parents in preindustrial agricultural and craft economies, this industrial context prompted laws limiting child labor. Modern adult work has become identified with alienation from our most creative, caring, and responsible selves. While the industrial era gave way to finance and technology, many of the same conditions of competition and alienation persist in adult jobs.

It is no wonder that young people seek sanctuary in the diversions of youth culture, resisting transition to such an alienated adulthood. But in truth they have little choice in the matter. Today, adolescence is a prolonged state of limbo in which youth are expected to prepare for adult work and future social significance — compensated for their loss of status with entertaining electronic and commodity distractions. Today, adolescence — as a preparatory stage for alienating adult work — does not normally allow young people to discover the intrinsic goodness of work, including work on behalf of God and neighbor, as did many former generations and other cultures. The popular assumption that young people should first learn correct ideas as a prelude to acting in the world ignores the important influence of work — that young people learn inestimably from active exploration of their world and their own energies in that world. Without such creative work some young people never find their signature gifts or hear God's call to vocation. Unfortunately, many youth ministers, taking cues from contemporary culture, neglect the formative influence of engaging young people in exploring their faith in active love of God and neighbor. As a result, youth miss the growth in faith that comes from acting on God's behalf in the world.

Through unreflective use in our youth ministry programs of "cultural technologies" (by this I mean not simply electronics, but also modes of entertainment or social institutions that leave young people passive), we are supporting a status quo that prefers that our young people sleep, and does not want them to become compassionate or intelligent enough to mobilize a challenge to its hegemony — which is precisely what the reign of God calls us to do. When wrapped in these cultural forms, the gospel itself is at risk of being subsumed by popular culture and reduced to something easily consumable — something compatible with the values of the middle class or its version of adolescence that requires no response to a broken world. Sometimes it seems as if we assume that the gospel of Jesus is too difficult to swallow without sensational embellishments — like a bitter pill that requires a spoonful of sugar to go down. The irony is that this difficult gospel of Jesus requires the active engagement of our whole selves — heart, mind, soul, and body — and is precisely what our youth yearn for. As ministers of the gospel, we cannot simply replicate in our youth programs contemporary modes of adolescence, including popular entertainment, pacifying modes of education, or exploitative employment that shape youth as passive consumers, but we must invite youth to the way of Jesus that requires awakening them to their full being.

Ironically, youth today have more income and distractions at their disposal than ever before in history and yet seem more dissatisfied. While some are lulled to sleep by the pacifying system of commodity consumption, many youth can still feel the stirring of their hearts yearning for faithful action. Youth whisper their secret to those who will hear, "We want to do something — to impact the world with our full powers and gifts."

Theological clues for a spirituality of action

Although the contemporary church has largely remained silent about the cultural expectation that young people remain passive, Christian theology has consistently held the importance of acting in creative and caring ways in the world. For some Christians, their faith has become an inert identity or possession that only perpetuates their slumber, suppressing any response to the beauty or brokenness of the world. But at the very heart of Christian theology we are reminded of God's own work in creating the world and reconciling and empowering us as partners in creating and healing. A Christian spirituality of work begins with an awareness of God's own activity in creation, including the following characteristics.

Authenticity

Creation is a product of God's own authenticity, not determined by any external laws or forces. So human work should include the possibility of authenticity — growing from our yearnings for beauty, justice, and goodness in the world, not the external pressure to pursue financial gain. If our work, like God's work in creation, embodies our authentic passions and commitments, then these will be continually cultivated and strengthened within us and in the world. The encyclical of Pope John Paul II, *Laborem Exercens,* observes that "when a man works, he not only alters things and society, he develops himself as well. He learns much, he cultivates his resources, he goes outside of himself. Rightly understood, this kind of growth is of greater value than any external riches which can be garnered."[1]

Beauty

God was pleased with creation and derived joy from its beauty. God's work in creation did not merely give shape to functioning systems, but wove into creation a surprising beauty and goodness. The structures of nature serve not only preservation of individuals and species, but also display of nature's riches. Human life is greatly enhanced by the beauty of God's creation and greatly diminished when this beauty is destroyed. Human work ought to embody aesthetic and ethical concerns for harmony, unity, diversity, and proportionality.

Relationality

God did not create discrete entities, but webs of interrelated and interdependent human and nonhuman life. God created a world in which Adam and Eve drew life from the bounty of the garden, and in turn cultivated the garden and cared for creatures. Not only were they created in need of relationships with creatures, but also with the Creator. An important rhythm of their lives included God's movement in the garden in the cool of the day. The original blessings of the garden were drawn from right relationships, while the subsequent curse was a result of a failure to respect and maintain these relationships rightly — through mistrust, secrecy, selfishness, dishonesty, and blame. *Laborem Exercens* asserts that in addition to providing the substance of life, through our work we are charged with the Christian duty of performing activities that benefit society and all creation. In so doing we, "are unfolding the Creator's work, consulting the advantages of their brothers and sisters, and contributing by their personal industry to the realization of the divine plan."[2]

Priority of life

God breathed life into creation, generating and sustaining life. The act of breathing life into creation indicates God's investment in creation and the holiness that resides in all of creation. This perspective on God-breathed creation disqualifies any view of creation as mere dead material for our thoughtless production or consumption. Reverence for God as the source of life requires us to view our work as participating with God in enlivening the world. In the view of some, life is but a veil of suffering to be endured, but God's validation of the goodness of this world requires us to respect and celebrate life and work amid creation.

Restful rhythms

God's work in creating the world has a Sabbath rhythm woven into it. So should our work provide time to step out of good work, in order to acknowledge God's role in our life among us. The Sabbath includes the sense that work and rest are not to be distinguished too discretely but are to be considered as integral to creative action. Work that does not include Sabbath risks alienating our bodies from our hearts, minds, and souls. By failing to remember God's presence in the suffering and bliss around us, we risk the possibility that our work may serve purposes other than God's, which may fragment the beauty and integrity that God intends for creation.

A christology of action

God's creative work continues in the work of Jesus and the Spirit. Not only does Christian theology offer a glimpse into the nature of God's good work, but also points to our empowerment for that work. Theologian Karl Barth understood God's work of reconciliation as the event in which Christ objectively reconciled the world to God, but also illuminates the Spirit's work, awakening us from our slumber and empowering us as partners with God. Barth's view of the offices of Christ provides a helpful way of considering how human activity can be connected to God's work in the world. The work of Christ entails a threefold movement in which humanity's justification, sanctification, and vocation are established. First, Christ in his priestly office descends from the bosom of God into the heart of humanity, sin, and death, wherein the objective justification of humanity was accomplished. Second, Christ, in his kingly office, ascends to the Godhead as an exalted human, wherein the objective sanctification of humanity was established. Third, Christ, as the God-human in his prophetic office, moves outward, mediating reconciliation by proclaiming its truth for all, thereby establishing the objective vocation of humanity. We can thus identify a Christian spirituality of work as involving the following characteristics.

Partnership with God

The work of the Holy Spirit is to establish within the sphere of human reality that which has been objectively accomplished in Christ. The Holy Spirit is the movement of God in which the church is awakened to, centered in, and gathered around the coming of Christ; is quickened or built up into an empowered and faithful community; and is sent out to participate in the consummation of the reign of God. Individually, the Holy Spirit is the movement of God in which, first, persons are awakened to one's justification in Christ; second, persons are empowered into a sanctified and fully alive humanity; and third, persons are also sent out to participate in the coming of the consummated reign of God. Christian growth and sanctification happen as individuals increasingly conform from within to our true being in partnership with the Spirit.

Overcoming the sin of sloth

Whereas the first work of the Spirit is awakening us to God's love, thus overcoming our sin of pride, the sin of sloth (inertia or sluggishness) is illuminated in the light of Christ's second exalting or empowering work. Sloth is a form of sin that stands in marked contrast to the assertive and aggressive sin of pride by which sin is usually defined. As such, theologians often overlook sloth. Sloth is the sin of failing to live as a fully alive and exalted human being. In the more fantastic sin of pride, humanity is ever in need of being humbled, while in the quiet sin of sloth, humanity is ever in need of being exalted. Sloth can be described alternately as the sin of not following the Spirit's direction; of not being a living self, a person not in relationship with others; or of allowing oneself to be powerless.

The eschatological character of human work

The one work of Christ's reconciliation has a third movement, beyond justification and sanctification. Christ's movement in the world extends outward to vocation as the Spirit invites reconciled humanity into this work of reconciling all of creation in God's exaltation. An understanding of Christian existence limited to these two movements of justification and sanctification results in a self-oriented, bourgeois, and this-worldly form of Christianity.[3] Barth insists that this future orientation in hope, and the fulfillment of one's vocation in light of it, is the primary theme of the Christian, the other two being secondary. Christian life is decidedly eschatological. The movement of the Spirit is toward that day when all of humanity shall be healed and reconciled in Christ. The world remains darkened by sin and brokenness, cruelty, oppression, injustice, and inhumanity, distant from that triumphant kingdom when all of creation shall be reconciled to one another and to God. Those who know God work toward this future, seeking participation with the Spirit who is ushering in its coming.

A contemplative spirituality of action

While Karl Barth's theology gives us important clues as to the nature of Christ's reconciling work in the world, there is a risk in his model that we might understand the Spirit's work as limited to motivating us for partnership in God's work — that work is but a product of spiritual life. But work is not only a product of the Spirit's motivation;

it is a means through which God moves us and provides an important means for spiritual growth. According to *Laborem Exercens,* "work helps all people to come closer ... to God, the Creator and Redeemer, to participate in his salvific plan for man and the world and to deepen their friendship with Christ in their lives by accepting, through faith, a living participation in his threefold mission as priest, prophet and king."[4] Work or activity is not simply a product of faith, but is also a spiritual means for fostering faith.

When we think of spirituality, the practices of prayer, silence, and solitude typically come to mind. And certainly, in today's frenetic world, practices of prayer and silence are enormously important for us to center ourselves in God's love, but we should not make the mistake of imagining these forms of spirituality as separate from action. In Parker Palmer's book *The Active Life,* Palmer describes his own search for an appropriate spirituality.[5] Upon emerging into adulthood during the 1960s and taking his place in the world of work, parenthood, and community responsibility, somewhere along the line Palmer began to fear the world with its demands, its assaults on his sense of competence and self-worth, and its threats of failure. As a response to this fear, he embarked on a spiritual journey into the world of contemplation — away from the world of action. After his own ten-year journey in a community governed by monastic norms, Palmer concluded:

> I do not thrive on the monastic virtues of stability, centeredness, balance. As much as I may need those qualities in my life, the words do not name those moments when I feel most alive and most able to share life with others. I thrive on the vitality and variety of the world of action. I value spontaneity more than predictability, exuberance more than order, inner freedom more than the authority of tradition, the challenge of dialogue more than the guidance of a rule, eccentricity more than staying on dead center.[6]

Palmer acknowledges the dangers that can be done by action and the importance of good guidance, but he also deeply appreciates and respects these energies. "To name them, I believe, is to name the living God — who has many names."[7] Parts of our spiritual tradition view these energies of work and activity as wild horses to be brought under control rather than life-giving streams that flow from the source. Alternately, he insists that

> the core message of all the great spiritual traditions is "Be not afraid." Rather, be confident that life is good and trustworthy. In this light, the great failure is not that of leading a full and vital active life, with all the mistakes and suffering such a life will bring (along with its joys). Instead the failure is to withdraw fearfully from the place to which one is called, to squander the most precious of all our birthrights — the experience of aliveness itself.[8]

He argues that "we need a spirituality which affirms and guides our efforts to act in ways that resonate with our innermost being and reality, ways that embody the vitalities God gave us at birth, ways that serve the great work of justice, peace and love."[9] Palmer reminds us that the heart of the spiritual quest is to know "the rapture of being alive," and to allow that knowledge to transform us into celebrants, advocates, defenders of life wherever we find it.[10]

The active life also makes it possible for us to discover ourselves and our world, to test our powers, to connect with other beings, to co-create a common reality. Take away the opportunity to work, to create, or to care — as our society does to too many people — and you have deprived someone of a chance to feel fully human. While the risks of acting are many — including egotism, pride, foolishness, fear of failure, appearing incompetent, criticism, or anger — it is even sadder to see people who have forfeited, or been denied, the chance to act with strength — and the sense of self that comes as we declare and discover our own truth through the active life.[11]

Both contemplation and action have at their root the ceaseless drive to be fully alive. Palmer says:

> Through action we both express and learn something of who we are, of the kind of world we have or want. Action, like

a sacrament, is the visible form of an invisible spirit, an outward manifestation of an inward power.... As we act, we not
only express what is in us and help give shape to the world; we
also receive what is outside us, and we reshape our inner selves.
When we act, the world acts back, and we and the world are
co-created.[12]

Even the failures of the active life open us to find the self that
remains hidden when we feel confident and secure, the seeking self
that draws us into the human adventure. The greatest risk in action is
the risk of self-revelation, and that is also action's greatest joy. When
we act, something of our inner mystery often emerges. To act is to
learn by doing. In this sense, acting is a contemplative practice: it
opens another way of exposing multiform truth — another means of
discernment.

Conclusion

Young people yearn to "do something" and so are expressing a holy
desire to engage meaningfully in the reconciliation of the world and
their true selves — beyond the frivolous social and recreational activities we provide in hopes of retaining their interest. They yearn
to be actors in history and not simply acted upon. Youth sense that
the world is filled with wounds for which they have resources. Youth
yearn to break free from the pacifying slumber of adolescence to engage the world as agents of faith, to participate with the God of Jesus
Christ in redeeming life within the bounds of history, space, and time.
    We must acknowledge the constraints of our culture that limit the
faithful agency of youth. Any youth ministry that seeks to take seriously its mission grounded in the threefold mission of Christ must
work contrary to a culture that seeks to keep young people passive.
If youth ministry is to be in partnership with the Spirit in reconciling
all creation in God's glory, we cannot consider the social construction of this passive adolescence as the final word. By unreflectively

participating in the institution of adolescence as a largely preparatory or passive stage of life, we are ignoring our theological clues for
full Christian life. By limiting the movements of young people and
relegating them to marginal, entertaining, or patronizing activities in
the church, we are denying them an important means of spiritual
growth, and we are denying them the means for exploring their best
selves and the hidden wholeness of the world. If our ministry with
youth corresponds to Christ's priestly, kingly, and prophetic offices, it
should involve a range of activities — including those that help them
to discover anew God's love for them, respond to God's love in ways
that elicit their best gifts, and seek to reconcile the vast brokenness
in the world.

Practices of acting

By engaging young people in faithful action, we are inviting them
to respond creatively to the broken dimensions of their lives and the
world and to the vision of God's promised wholeness, unfolding in
their experiences and reflections. In the discernment process we have
described in previous chapters, youth engage in listening to their fears
and hopes, wounds and blessings, cries of suffering and celebration.
Second, they investigate the world in which these wounds and blessings have erupted — and the social, political, cultural, and economic
forces that shape them. Third, they focus these themes prayerfully and
theologically, seeking ways of connecting their stories to the story
of God. These three processes help clarify for young people God's
call to action in the world. In particular, the guiding question for
this acting movement in discernment is, "How does listening to and
understanding the experiences of youth, and listening to God and
dreaming God's dream of an alternate future, call young people to
respond actively in the world?"

Engaging in faithful action requires a series of six steps:

1. clarifying aims of action
2. brainstorming

3. judging

4. planning

5. implementation

6. evaluation

While these steps are often legitimately collapsed or accomplished in various ways, they represent important dimensions of engaging youth in action.

Clarifying aims

In previous movements of listening, understanding and remembering/ dreaming, youth have focused upon particular experiences of brokenness or glory in the world. The possibilities for focusing action include not only addressing the chosen theme and its situation, but also the root causes that have surfaced in the course of the critical and theological study. At times it is important to distinguish superficial causes of problems from the root cause of a problem. To create remedies or solutions without understanding and engaging root problems may simply prolong or perpetuate the identified problem. For example, offering food to a homeless person is an important act of charity, but understanding the roots of homelessness may lead us to seek a greater justice engaging other problems — joblessness, rental policies, bank redlining, inadequate welfare policies, or globalization that prevent people from climbing out of poverty. Most often, problems are so complex as to require multiple levels of action.

As a step in preparing for appropriate action, it can be helpful to reframe all previous reflections on direct and indirect causes as aims for action. Identifying aims also ensures that action projects follow in a natural way from their reflections. Invite youth to create a set of aims in response to the following question: "*Given the ways our hearts have been drawn to particular situations, and our minds have discovered more about these situations, and our souls help us to grasp God's work in the world, we can participate with God in the world's healing by aiming to* _____ ." This sentence can help young people focus their actions in response to their critical and theological reflections. Aims may not include concrete actions, but should describe what these actions seek to accomplish. Aims include statements like, "We aim to break our addiction to media culture, live more simply, create more just structures to help the poor, heal environmental degradation, provide opportunities for our church to be better neighbors in our community, better integrate youth in the worship of our congregation, or to foster improved relationships with adults in our church." Creating such a list of aims helps youth focus their action in ways that directly relate to their reflections.

Brainstorming

Once youth have surfaced the aims of their action, invite them to engage in a session of creative brainstorming about possible responses to situations they have studied. At this stage, brainstorming should be open and free, with minimal thought of financial or practical concerns. Brainstorming should engage youth in creating specific actions that address the particular aims they have surfaced.

Remind youth that they may respond on various levels — individually, communally, culturally, politically, or economically. For example, if young people explore "the exploitation of young people by corporate media," possible responses include

- individuals boycotting media products

- youth groups creating a covenant to hold each other accountable for the disciplined use of media

- youth groups committing themselves in prayer for young people and those exploiting them

- youth groups mobilizing congregations and communities to lobby Congress or corporations about their exploitation of youth

- youth groups creating their own music recordings to share among themselves

While these do not exhaust the possibilities, they illuminate possible responses that involve individuals, youth groups, congregations, communities, and larger political bodies.

The following is a simple procedure for engaging a group in brainstorming possible actions.[13]

- Chairs are set in one large circle so that everyone can see and hear everyone else.

- The middle of the circle is empty and open.

- There are no tables or podiums, but there are half sheets of flipchart paper and markers on the floor in the center.

- The facilitator has posted the aims that have surfaced in their earlier reflections.

- The group of youth or youth and adults sitting in the circle are asked to consider the list of aims, and when they feel moved to respond to a particular aim to rise and write the aim on a piece of paper and post it on the wall. One by one, or all at once, other youth or adults should rise to identify a particular aim they are interested in brainstorming about for the next hour to hour and a half, and to tape their paper on the wall around the room. Their announcement and postings signal their intention to facilitate a discussion on this aim and its potential ways to take action.

- When all the aims for discussion and their discussion leaders have been identified, the facilitator instructs the whole group to move to sign up for the discussions they want to attend. Depending on the number of aims and the time allotted for this process, a schedule should be constructed that makes time for all of the aims that have been selected. Ideally, a whole day or weekend should be given to this creative process, depending upon the number of aims the group has surfaced earlier.

- The large circle is then broken into many small circles in the corners of the room or in separate breakout spaces. Each group is working on some important aim, creating ideas about action projects for the youth group or congregation. Every session has been proposed by someone who really cares about that aim and has taken responsibility for making sure it gets addressed. The convener is also responsible for recording the action ideas and conclusions reached in his or her session.

- As the first sessions finish, at roughly the scheduled time, the second sessions begin. If the work isn't finished, it continues or a sequel is scheduled.

- At the conclusion of the day or at a particular scheduled time, the large group joins together again to hear the reports of the small groups. An alternative is for the plenary group to migrate from space to space in which groups have posted their newsprint ideas to hear each report from the group's working space.

Judging

Once youth have exhausted their ideas for how to engage the situations at hand, they will be ready to make some judgments about which ideas may be most appropriate for their action. As groups and individuals are preparing for some faithful action, it is important that the action remain true to their understandings of the problem, their passion around the issues, and their faith. In the 1960s, during the civil rights movement, Rev. Martin Luther King Jr. and his followers made a conscious decision to not act violently, but instead decided that their actions should be consistent with their faith commitments to the nonviolent way of Jesus. Their actions were the result of passionate, intelligent, theological, faithful, and strategic decisions. The decision to march to Montgomery, for example, was based on a number of factors, including determinations about the most effective and faithful ways to speak truth to power.

Walter Wink's work on the third way of Jesus Christ suggests that Jesus called his disciples neither to violence nor passivity, but to a third type of action. Wink describes Jesus's action as bearing resemblance to the martial art jujitsu, in which the weight of the aggressor is used against him or her. For example, Jesus's admonition to "turn the other cheek" was not advocating passivity. While it was common to hit a slave with the back of the hand (or on the left cheek), Jesus instead recommended a response that called for the victim to insist that aggressor strike instead with the palm of the hand (or the right cheek) — the one reserved for equals. Many of our patterns of interaction promote viewing the other person as an object. Jesus advocated action that called the aggressor to view the other as a human subject. Great care should be taken to ensure that action projects invite others to view young people as living agents with gifts, wisdom, and contributions to God's reign.

Judging the most appropriate action involves not only engaging theological criteria but also prayerfully seeking God. Quakers often utilize group consensus and silence as a means for allowing God to speak. Below is a brief description of Quaker process.

Quaker consensus building

Decision-making groups can use the "Quaker Process." This process, introduced earlier, is based on a theological assumption that God is present in the decision-making group and is equally accessible by every member of the group. The group seeks unity by seeking a decision ("sense of the meeting") consistent with the promptings of God. The group becomes wiser than the individual because it partakes of the wisdom of all its members empowered by the Spirit. The aim of a meeting is to seek the will of God. It is not a matter of bowing to the will of the majority, as Friends do not vote. Consensus building involves an exercise of listening to God through what each person says. Responsibilities of the facilitator include the following actions:

- conducting the meeting

- discerning "the sense of the meeting"

- offering a minute that encapsulates what has gone before and recording any decision that has been arrived at, if an item has been thoroughly considered

- attuning to the tenor and tone of the discussion, and perhaps calling for a period of silence if discussion seems bogged down or overly contentious
- encouraging reluctant speakers or reining in participants who speak too frequently or put forward their opinions without regard to others
- if no decision can be reached, helping the group figure out what action is called for (e.g., a committee, further study)
- communicating the group's decisions to the community, including the circulation of written minutes

The group members have the responsibility to enter into the process, to speak up as needed, to keep to the topic at hand, to be clear about objections, to adhere to the principles set out above, and to use the silence for guidance and centering. This process leads to unity. The whole group weaves a decision; although individuals may not agree with every point, they recognize the wisdom of the group's decision and agree to support it. This process allows for one individual to "stand in the way" of a decision if he or she thinks it is wrong. However, it also allows for that individual to "stand aside" despite objections, if he or she feels that is better for the group. The latter course of action is the one most frequently used by dissenters in Quaker settings. The agreement to support a decision once made is crucial. Objections should be raised and heard in the meeting, not afterward; otherwise, the unity of the group is false and the decision undermined.

Planning

Once youth have agreed on actions they wish to take, more detailed planning is often required. Groups should determine in concrete terms what they are doing, when, where, and what resources are required. Some considerations for planning may include:

- What are the aims we hope to accomplish?
- What is the action?

- What are the times and dates for the action?

- What kinds of communications may be required for its success?

- What kinds of financial resources may be needed?

- What human resources may be needed?

- What material resources may be needed?

- What transportation may be required?

- What other kinds of support may be needed — prayer, covenant agreements, cooperation with other groups?

- What are the costs of being involved in this action?

- What are the benefits of being involved in this action?

If the action to be taken requires cooperation among the youth group, then it is important to invite input from the youth and continually test their investment in the project. It may be helpful for young people to create a covenant that holds each other accountable for actions to which they have committed themselves.

Implementation

If young people have accomplished their critical and theological reflection and have judged that their action is consistent with God's call in the world, these reflections can give their work a passion that is missing from much youth activity. As the action project is being implemented, it is important to remind the youth of their reflections and passions that led them to this action. Art can be an important reminder of the significance of an action. Some groups have found ways to codify their themes, as pictures, photos, or songs. Through singing, drawing, painting, or drama, for example, young people can distill the salient parts of their critical and theological reflection as a way of reminding them of the importance of their action. A Bible verse or theological idea can provide helpful support to their action — and helps young people keep before them how this action connects them to God's story. Two young girls in Oregon, as a result of their study about food, wrote a humorous song making fun of junk food.

They sang their funny song about the dangers of junk food and young people's addictions to it as a way of reminding themselves and others of the importance of their action.

Evaluation

As young people are engaging in faithful action in the world, they should consider all of their reflections and actions as provisional. Christian discipleship can be understood as giving as much of ourselves as we understand to as much of God as we understand each day, and it is important to continually expand our understanding and responses throughout our lives. No set of reflections on a theme can fully encompass the richness of lived reality. Our perceptions of God's work in the world are also provisional and subject to correction or addition. We should therefore remain open to learning from our actions. It is vital that we learn from engaging in action, and to view these learnings as ways that God is creating us as whole selves — hearts, minds, souls, and bodies. Questions that we might ask as we debrief any action include, "What new tensions, passions, celebrations, or conflicts do you notice? What new insights about the world and this situation do you learn? Has this experience provoked new insights about God and God's work in the world? What other thoughts do you have about ways to engage this theme or concern?"

One story of action

In previous chapters, we observed how one group of young people explored the statement and situation, "Some African American males are angry because of unfair treatment in the juvenile justice system." When they *listened* to their hearts — through conversation, timed writing, prayer, drama, and art — they discovered a common tension that they lived with in their community. When they engaged this theme, analyzing it with their minds — through empirical studies, conversations with experts, reading, Internet research, and dramatic representations — they gained a significant degree of *understanding* about the causes for the theme and its situations. And in their process of *remembering* and *dreaming* they learned of God's love for all people and desire that they be free from persecution and harassment.

In exploring their particular situation, they learned that their experience was only one dimension of a systemic problem of how law enforcement and justice systems relate to black men. They also learned that young black men are overrepresented in the justice and prison system in the United States, as a result of a number of factors, including structural racism and poverty that prevents young black men from having access to the same legal representation as white youth.

In a lengthy discussion of how to respond to these pervasive structures, this group of youth debated a range of options. They decided to respond in several ways: (1) They mobilized a group of young students to protest at city hall the recent shooting death of a young black boy by a police officer, (2) and they agreed to start "Teen Courts" in their own high schools. Teen Courts are a recent invention of a California attorney who learned that the recidivism rate of juvenile justice systems in California topped 91 percent. He arranged for juvenile judges to organize high school classes as juvenile courts for first-time offenders. In Teen Courts, high school students, for academic credit, learn about the roles and processes of court and serve as attorneys, jurors, and judges for first-time offenders. Teen Court participants across the United States report that recidivism rates for juvenile offenders are cut at least in half in comparison to the juvenile justice system.[14] The young people discerning the theme, "Some African American males are angry because of unfair treatment in the juvenile justice system," enacted their faith by starting Teen Courts in their high schools to create a fairer environment for young black offenders.

Other examples of actions taken by youth are as follows:

- Resisting the blatant exploitation of the music industry by creating their own music recordings for sharing among themselves and their community.

- Creating educational videos to inform churches about issues of youth sexuality and gender inequality.

- Painting murals and performing plays that help communities to reenvision their roles in the community.

- Challenging the church pastor to include more of youth experience in sermon illustrations.

- Challenging the worship committee to fully integrate young people into Sunday liturgy and reshape worship to be more youth friendly.

- Planning and implementing a neighborhood celebration to introduce neighbors to each other and the resources of the church.

The intrinsic goodness of action

In utilizing this fourth approach with youth groups over many years, I have found that the fruits of action are among the most tangible rewards. For young people who have been relegated to institutions in which they have less than full power, exercising the powers of their hearts, minds, and souls — culminating in the mobilization of their bodies as creative agents in the world — is enormously empowering. Young people are surprised by the delight of using their intellects and bodies as agents of change. They find that taking action is surprisingly satisfying and qualitatively unlike those pleasures provided by popular entertainment. Many young people report feeling like "they are being used by God to change the world," or "God is working through me."

Unlike work for money, schoolwork in preparation for making money, or other utilitarian pursuits, work that has grown out of their own passion and reflections of the world has its own intrinsic value and delight. This kind of work makes youth hunger for Frederick Buechner's description of vocation as "where our deep gladness meets the world's deep hunger." Especially if their actions are sponsored and validated by adults and faith communities, these experiences give young people a taste of Christian discipleship in its fullest sense — of following God.

Unlike youth discipleship programs that perpetually prepare youth for a future discipleship, this approach engages young people in a process that continually seeks fuller experiences of their hearts, minds, souls, and bodies in relationship to God and this broken world. This holistic approach to youth discipleship engages young people in their prophetic vocation as youth, resisting those structures of adolescence that seek to pacify and domesticate them. And like the awakening kiss of Sleeping Beauty, becoming agents of faith in the world awakens young people to new possibilities for faithfulness and vitality.

Notes

1. Pope John Paul II, *Laborem Exercens,* papal encyclical on human work, September 14, 1981, 26.5.

2. Ibid., 25.4.

3. "It is still too true in that tradition (in which the Christian life was limited to justification and sanctification) that the being of humanity in Jesus Christ has as such a very this-worldly, immanentist, even middle-class appearance." Karl Barth, *Church Dogmatics,* 4 vols., trans. G. T. Thompson (Edinburgh: T & T Clark, 1936–77), 4/1:109.

4. Pope John Paul II, *Laborem Exercens,* 24.2.

5. Parker Palmer, *The Active Life: A Spirituality of Work, Creativity, and Caring* (San Francisco: Jossey-Bass, 1999).

6. Ibid., 4.

7. Ibid., 7.

8. Ibid., 8.

9. Ibid., 9.

10. Ibid., 8.

11. Ibid., 21.

12. Ibid., 17.

13. Michael Herman, "Working in Open Space: A Guided Tour." See his Web site at www.openspaceworld.org/wiki/wiki/wiki.cgi.

14. Jeffrey A. Butts, Jeneen Buck, and Mark B. Coggeshall, "The Impact of Teen Court on Young Offenders." Research Report, a study of the Urban Institute Justice Policy Center, April 2002.

Eight

Appropriating discernment for ministry with youth

In this book I have suggested a set and flow of activities that constitute a practice of discernment as an approach to congregational youth ministry. My hope is that young people internalize such practices of discernment and that these practices help them discern the call of God throughout their lives.

I have argued that the institution of adolescence, especially in the United States, is domesticated — that young people are alienated from their own hearts, minds, souls, and bodies; from the adults in their communities; and hence from the conditions required to fully explore their own giftedness. I have also raised suspicions that some popular forms of youth ministry have contributed to this domestication. Therefore, in this final chapter, I want to suggest ways of appropriating these rhythms of discernment — listening, understanding, remembering/dreaming, and acting — for youth ministry, as a means of connecting young people to their own powers, and the power of God, restoring their charisms within the community for the reign of God.

I want to begin by acknowledging that these rhythms already play significant roles in most youth ministry. Youth ministers routinely create Bible studies or youth talks based on their practice of listening to young people and the themes of their lives. Most youth curriculum in some way engages in analysis of some social issue and frames it theologically. And most youth groups actively engage in missions work, whether journeying to Mexico or Appalachia or to nearby centers for ministries with the homeless and poor. Yet, despite the presence of these habits in popular youth ministry, they remain unrelated and discrete, and the responsibility for these habits lies largely in the hands of adults. While these common youth ministry activities are at present enormously beneficial, by making them more deliberate, connecting them to each other, and placing responsibility for them in the hands of youth, this discernment approach to youth ministry can provide the additional benefits outlined below.

The benefits

Fostering grassroots responsibility for youth ministry

The practice of discernment strengthens connections between activities that in popular youth ministry often remain largely unconnected: connecting listening to the stories of youth with critical and theological study; connecting study with prayer; connecting study and prayer with action; and connecting action again to listening, studying, and praying. Viewing these activities as isolated and discrete has several negative effects: it builds largely upon the interests and commitments of youth ministers, curriculum publishers, or other adults — and not on those of youth. It perpetuates youth ministry as a top-down enterprise, always driven by adults. But connecting these activities helps to build youth ministry on the interests and commitments of youth and fosters grassroots momentum and responsibility.

Cultivating worldview and identity

Isolating as discrete from one another the activities of listening, understanding, dreaming, and acting inhibits young people from making the necessary connections to form working theories of the world and God's work in it. According to Erik Erikson, one of the tasks of adolescence is achieving identity. Identity is achieved as young people — through an ideological perspective or a worldview — gain a greater sense of how the world coheres. The practice of discernment outlined in this volume fosters habits of questioning and making connections that are crucial for constructing communal and individual perspectives, thus forming a cohesive identity and faith that is historically meaningful.

Grounding youth ministry in the natural curiosity of youth

The practice of discernment removes the sole responsibility for critical and theological study from the youth minister and grounds it instead in the natural curiosity of young people. There is much evidence that adolescents are developmentally equipped to make connections that enhance their understanding of the world, yet many adults assume as normal apathy among youth. While it is true that consumer culture mutes the natural curiosity of youth, and many high schools also fail to enhance this natural hunger, so do many congregations by viewing youth ministry solely as passing on static traditions. The practice of raising questions and making connections through a discernment process encourages curiosity. Learning approaches that foster and build upon the natural curiosity of young people enjoy an advantage in opening youth to loving God with their minds.

Encouraging depth and complexity of reflections

Whereas, in much popular youth ministry, teaching that involves complexity is often seen as a necessary evil — which youth ministers and teachers must force or rush through, lest they strain the attentive capacities of young people — this approach exploits the intrinsic pleasure of learning about the world and God. When young people discover areas of their own interest, they are more eager to explore issues with depth and complexity. The practice of discernment, grounded on the commitment and curiosity of youth, fosters stronger intrinsic motivation to explore particular issues in greater depth and complexity.

Placing issues in local contexts

The practice of discernment makes adolescent life the curricular text and opens it for study, prayer, and action. The possibilities for problematizing contexts, issues, and themes are endless. The more local the issue, the more unique and rich your youth ministry will be. Simply living in particular contexts creates new situations that demand discernment, whereas popular youth ministry resources may miss the mark of what is relevant and energizing for the youth in your own community.

Involving issues that extend to adults

The practice of discernment moves beyond exploring the immediate questions of youth and involves issues of concern to the entire faith community. For example, exploring issues important to adolescents often involves examining cultural versions of success, consumerism, worker exploitation, and lifestyle choices that impact the environment and impoverished workers of developing countries. This approach to discernment compels young people to look beyond the circumscribed world of their high school peer groups and to grasp larger social contexts, structures, and systems. This kind of reflection is best done in conversation with adults, who provide greater expertise and without whose support young people cannot respond in fully faithful ways. Additionally, empowering young people for more significant social roles challenges structures currently controlled by adults. Changing them requires partnership with adults.

Creating knowledge

Whereas popular youth ministry has largely been founded on the presumption of the need to pass on information to youth, this discernment approach to youth ministry creates a conversation between adults, Christian tradition, and youth. As long as youth ministry is seen as the transmission of established ideas and practices, the only appropriate role for youth will be as passive consumers. However, if youth ministry can reframe its activities to make them more organically related, then it can reorient youth in conversation with Christian faith and the texts of their lives, opening them to more creative responses. Once their lives are viewed not simply as scripted, but as appropriated through critical reflection and constructive action, then young people can have a greater sense of their own power in shaping their lives in relation to their faith. Apart from these critical and constructive habits, young people risk cultivating faith that is too easily assimilated to dominant cultural views.

Forming habits for a lifetime

The practice of discernment engages young people in activities that are themselves important life skills. Whereas much popular youth ministry, through curriculum or youth talks, introduces youth to the perspectives of other people, this approach to discernment prepares youth to move into adulthood in a more active and reflective way by engaging them in habits of raising questions and making connections. As they learn to exegete their world and bring it into conversation with their faith, they are less likely to simply attach an impotent faith onto an unreflective life.

Organizing and embodying discernment

If we assume the above benefits accrue from the practice of discernment, then an important task of ministry with youth may be seen as creating space for the activities of listening, understanding, remembering and dreaming, and acting. Precisely how these rhythms are organized and embodied in congregations may vary greatly. Below are some options.

Exploratory groups

In this approach, entire youth groups may be broken into small groups around common interests for the purpose of exploring specific contexts or themes. For example, one church youth group divided into smaller subgroups to explore various contexts of adolescent life: home, church, school, peer groups, and work. Each small group of four to seven members was assigned one particular context to observe. Each week, after observing their particular context, these small groups came together with the plenary youth group to report the stories of the youth they observed. As each small group told stories of pain and joy in the lives of their peers, others from the plenary group were given a chance to add observations or challenge those of the group reporting. The conversations sparked from these observations were very rich.

A key purpose of these plenary discussions is to get a deeper sense of which stories or themes are commonly experienced or most deeply felt among youth. When young people begin discussing a theme that is common among them or felt deeply, there is a palpable rise of energy in the room, as everyone begins to talk at once. It is very important for adults or youth facilitators to notice when this happens and try to capture the issues with the most interest. These themes contain the most possibility of sustaining interest throughout processes of critical and theological reflection, and the motivation to mobilize youth to change their world.

Once the various small groups have reported over weeks and months on their contexts, and the whole youth group has acknowledged a few key themes around which there is energy and passion, several possibilities are available for exploring these themes in greater depth. One possibility is that youth might remain in the same small groups or alternately reorganize in different small groups focused around particular themes. In this case, small groups could continue to explore themes through critical and theological research that they could report back to the larger group. This would allow the larger plenary group to continue to interact with small groups, adding insights and questions, and sending the small groups back to explore questions in greater depth. The advantage of this model is that as small groups report and interact with each other, the large group is slowly drawing conclusions about how respective themes are related to those reported by other groups — giving group members an emerging map of their lives, revealing systems, structures, and dynamics that impact adolescent life in their particular community.

Working within existing structures

Another option for organizing youth ministry in the rhythms of discernment involves utilizing existing youth ministry structures. For example, many congregational youth ministries are organized around the formal structures of Sunday school, Bible study, fellowship gathering, retreats, and mission opportunities. Some youth groups I have worked with have chosen to adapt these structures by slightly changing the focus of these groups to involve the contextual themes that were earlier explored. For example, once a youth group has divided itself into small groups to explore adolescent life and contexts, then they may decide that Sunday night Youth Fellowship is an appropriate place for small groups to report and for plenary groups to engage these reports. Sunday school classes might be organized around exploring particular themes and their social or cultural causes. Bible study classes might become a place for youth to engage particular themes from the perspective of the Christian tradition — utilizing the traditional sources, including Bible studies, theological studies, or the history or the social principles of particular denominations. Periodic weekend retreats might include possibilities for more intensive prayer focused around these themes. Mission opportunities, sometimes focused on local issues and sometimes focused on needs from beyond local communities, might involve strategizing and planning to implement action projects that surface from various groups or plenary sessions.

Congregational discernment

Another option that some congregations have successfully utilized involves engaging the entire congregation in discernment. This option is perhaps best utilized by small or medium-size congregations that can fit into a single room for reflection and conversation. In this option, the pastor, youth minister, or another facilitator leads the congregation in exploring the themes of adolescent life. Some congregations have focused their observations on their experiences of youth within the life of the congregation — where and how they experience youth in their midst. This involves the entire congregation in exploring how they relate with youth. However, such conversations must also allow space for young people to report on their experiences of life beyond the congregation. If the church is to support the growth and faith of youth, they must have an appreciation for how youth experience their lives.

As entire congregations engage in the movements of listening, understanding, remembering/dreaming, and acting, they can begin to take greater responsibility for how they care for their youth and form them in faith. Instead of relegating youth ministry to a congregational ghetto — driven by youth ministry professionals or curriculum from the denominational office — the entire congregation can conceive of how to create an ethos of ministry with youth, a network of care that holds youth in the practices and ideas of faith, but also engages them in embodying the witness of Christ in their particular contexts.

How congregations decide to embody these movements is not as important as seeking to integrate them in ways appropriate to their context. In some cases, congregations, after much discernment, have decided to minimize the activities solely for youth, and maximize the intergenerational activities that put adults in relation with youth. Through their discernment, they found that young people and adults greatly benefited when they engaged together in activities of study and action. Each congregation needs to discern and explore options that seem most appropriate to its own context.

Discernment amid the constellation of practices

A question that arises frequently concerns how this approach to youth ministry relates to other practices that form youth in Christian faith. By emphasizing discernment, the point of this book is not to diminish the importance of forming young people in the foundational stories, ideas, and practices that describe a particular sort of God and life lived in response to this God. The ideas and practices of Christian faith are best communicated by an intergenerational community seeking to embody this life in a way that is compelling to young people, in ways that convey their love for God and neighbor. How we take food, show hospitality to strangers, forgive others, seek justice, care for the earth, work, play, worship, pray, organize households, give testimony, and discern the spirits all represent our commitments to God in a way that mere theological or biblical ideas cannot. There is a beauty in the whole Christian life that cannot be captured by mere ideas.

This ecology of Christian practices forms a context in which the practice of discernment is appropriately situated. Nevertheless, discernment — exploring truth about ourselves, our world, and God — is a central practice that alerts us to potential distortions in our other practices. For example, in recent years some women have alerted us to the ways in which traditional practices of organizing households have kept women in exclusively domestic roles, preventing their being appreciated in a range of roles. These conclusions were presumably reached through thoughtful and prayerful deliberation. Without engaging our hearts, minds, souls, and bodies in discernment, our lives become too easily assimilated to cultural norms that distort human life and relationships. But if discernment helps to clarify the shape of other practices, other practices also shape our experiences and sensibilities, which are fundamental to discernment. For example, those who ignore Christian practices that engage them in hospitality to the poor will not be moved in a way that compels them to explore the injustices that create poverty and discern God's direction for the church.

Despite the importance of a range of practices, rarely in history has there been a greater need for young people to discern the forces that seek to domesticate and exploit them. Rarely has there been a greater need for God's guidance in exploring their true vocation. Yet, just as surely as there are forces that domesticate youth, there are signs of hope — such as the Jesuit young people who gather each year to protest American military collaboration with tyrannical Latin American governments, the young people from across the globe who flock to Taizé to sing and pray, the young people who challenge forces of global capitalism that destroy indigenous cultures, and the young people who express their creativity in projects on behalf of the common good.

The question for the church is not whether God is at work in the world, but whether youth ministry will represent a witness for God or whether it will serve forces that distort humanity and creation's completion in the reign of God. Often, when I elaborate the ideas and practices of discernment as an approach to youth ministry, no one disputes their truth and importance, but some adult youth workers warn me that they will not work among average congregations and youth. Ironically, when I listen to young people express their yearnings for God, they express an eagerness to engage the gospel in all of its fullness. My guess is that the yearnings of young people are the deepest hopes of us all. We must open ourselves to these yearnings, to youth themselves, and to God's life living strongly in young people.